WASTE

WASTE

One Woman's Fight Against
America's Dirty Secret

Catherine Coleman Flowers
Foreword by Bryan Stevenson

THE
NEW
PRESS

NEW YORK
LONDON

Requests for permission to reproduce selections from this book should
be made through our website: https://thenewpress.com/contact.

Published in the United States by The New Press, New York, 2020
Distributed by Two Rivers Distribution

ISBN 978-1-62097-608-1 (hc)
ISBN 978-1-62097-609-8 (ebook)

CIP data is available

The New Press publishes books that promote and enrich public discussion and
understanding of the issues vital to our democracy and to a more equitable world.
These books are made possible by the enthusiasm of our readers; the support
of a committed group of donors, large and small; the collaboration of our many
partners in the independent media and the not-for-profit sector; booksellers, who
often hand-sell New Press books; librarians; and above all by our authors.

www.thenewpress.com

Composition by dix!
This book was set in Fairfield LH

Printed in the United States of America

4   6   8   10   9   7   5

For Taylor, K.J.,
and seven generations to come

Contents

Foreword

Our planet is dying. It is not a death from natural causes or some inevitable decline. Instead, we are slowly killing our future through greed, abuse of precious resources, reckless consumption, and irresponsible behavior. The environmental crisis—like most crises—will victimize the poor and vulnerable the most. In the United States, Black people, indigenous people, and communities of color will bear the heaviest burden of avoidable disease, degraded quality of life, and unnecessary suffering. This has sadly become the American story.

For too long, the impact of environmental neglect on the poor and people of color has gone unaddressed, which is why the advocacy of people like Catherine Flowers is so important. Policymakers in our nation are painfully ignorant about the multiple ways low-income communities suffer from avoidable illness. Elected officials who believe we eradicated hookworm infections in the U.S. decades ago know nothing about what we've documented in Lowndes County, Alabama. Our policy-makers have heard about asthma, lead poisoning, cancer, and a multitude of other sicknesses resulting from toxins, contaminants, and industrial waste, but there has been no appropriate response to the burden of these diseases on the poor. Our collective failure to invest in adequate sanitation, clean drinking water, and effective responses to pollution is taking life from the most vulnerable and marginalized among us.

In Alabama's rural Black Belt, the evidence of our neglect and exploitation of the poor can be seen everywhere. I met Catherine Flowers many years ago when impoverished Black residents in Lowndes County were being arrested and criminally prosecuted for not having functioning septic systems— even while being denied basic services and the infrastructure needed to install an effective system. It's a familiar dynamic Black people have endured since being forcibly trafficked to this continent from Africa. Policymakers create structural inequality and then criminalize those most burdened and at risk who fail to meet the demands of that structure.

The good news is that the work of Catherine Flowers demonstrates that there is more to this narrative. The children of the formerly enslaved in this region, the people terrorized by convict leasing and lynching, excluded by segregation and Jim Crow, don't just live in the rural South—they persist with an unparalleled determination to survive and fight for equality and fair treatment. It is critical that we understand their stories if we are to save our planet.

I grew up in a poor, racially segregated rural community. Managing wastewater was a long-term challenge in our home. My brother and I spent years pumping raw sewage onto the same backyard where we played football and baseball. Flushing a toilet, taking a shower or a bath was perilous and came with unknown hazards for the household. Some of our neighbors relied on outhouses with no indoor plumbing to manage. As I've grown older, I now realize that the worst part of these conditions is that we were made to believe that this is acceptable—just the way things are—in the wealthiest nation in the world.

It is this orientation to environmental abuse, this accommodation of poverty and racially biased management of toxins and contaminants, that may be the most insidious aspect of our current crisis. Too many believe that we have no choice; this is the best we can do. Catherine Flowers tells an important story and reminds us that we do have a choice, we can do better.

Over the last thirty years, a movement has emerged to change the way we talk and think about environmental justice. Environmentalists have not always been as responsive to the perspective of the poor and the impact of environmental abuse on communities of color but through tireless advocacy and important work like the efforts detailed in this book, that is changing. There is a new chapter in the quest for environmental justice that is long overdue. America's dirty secret is a secret no more and I pray that we all have the courage to act and to save the Earth's most precious possession, its people.

Bryan Stevenson

WASTE

Chapter 1

My story starts in Lowndes County, Alabama, a place that's been called "Bloody Lowndes" because of its violent, racist history. It's part of Alabama's Black Belt, a broad swath of rich, dark soil worked and inhabited largely by poor Black people who, like me, are descendants of slaves. Our ancestors were ripped from their homes and brought here to pick the cotton that thrived in the fertile earth.

I grew up here, left to get an education, and followed a range of professional opportunities. But something about that soil gets in your blood. I came back with hopes of helping good, hard-working people rise up out of the poverty that bogs them down like Alabama mud. Little did I know that the soil itself would lead me to my life's mission.

A big part of my work now is educating people about rural poverty and environmental injustice—how poor people are trapped in conditions no one else would put up with, both in Alabama and around the United States. Those conditions— polluted air, tainted water, untreated sewage—make people sick. They make it hard for children to thrive and adults to succeed. I tell people about the ways climate change is making those conditions even worse, and even more widespread, and that now they're starting to afflict people who aren't used to that kind of misery. I speak to audiences around the country and even abroad.

But when I'm home in Alabama, I take people to see such conditions for themselves. We visit families crowded into run-down homes where no one should have to live, where people lack heat in the winter and plumbing in all seasons. We visit homes in the country with no means of wastewater treatment, because septic systems cost more than most people earn in a year and tend to fail anyway in the impervious clay soil. Families cope the best they can, mainly by jerry-rigging PVC pipe to drain sewage from houses and into cesspools outside. In other words, what goes into their toilets oozes outside into the woods or yards, where children and pets play. Pools of waste form breeding grounds for parasites and disease.

Moving to town isn't necessarily a solution. We meet families who pay for wastewater treatment in the towns where they live, only to have raw sewage back up into their homes, saturating rugs and carpets, whenever it rains—and it rains a lot in Alabama.

We see firsthand the conditions that led to a resurgence of hookworm, an energy-sapping tropical parasite that northern newspaper headlines called "the germ of laziness" in the early twentieth century when it was rampant in the South. It was considered eradicated by mid-century, when indoor plumbing was commonplace. Nobody gave it much thought until a few years ago. That's when I convinced tropical disease experts to test Lowndes County residents for parasites, and they found that hookworm was back. That finding was ominous because Lowndes County isn't unique in its poverty or its geography. No one knows yet how far the hookworm infestation has spread.

Before I take anyone to Lowndes County, we start in nearby Montgomery, the state capital and one-time capital of the Confederacy, with a history lesson. Maybe it's the former history teacher in me, but I believe that you can't understand how rural Alabama wound up with raw sewage in people's yards without first learning about how African Americans were brought here as slaves to work the soil.

In the eighteenth and nineteenth centuries, Montgomery was a hub for the domestic slave trade, largely because cotton in those days was such a labor-intensive crop and grew so well here. The clay soil holds water better than it drains it, keeping the roots of the cotton plant well hydrated. What was good for cotton turned out not to be so good for plumbing, as we'll see later.

Today, reminders of the slave trade and Alabama's racist history appear all around downtown Montgomery. The First White House of the Confederacy, where Jefferson Davis lived briefly in 1861, is a tourist spot on Washington Avenue now. Then there's the white-columned capitol, where Governor George Wallace famously declared in his 1963 inaugural speech, "Segregation now, segregation tomorrow, segregation forever."

Some landmarks of the old South and Jim Crow era have taken on a whole new life. There's the old Greyhound station, where a mixed-race group of mostly young people called Freedom Riders stepped off a bus they'd boarded to protest segregation on public transit and into a violent mob in 1961. Now it's the Freedom Rides Museum. The Rosa Parks Museum stands on Montgomery Street, where Parks was arrested in 1955 for refusing to give up her seat on a city bus to a white man.

On Commerce Street, the former site of holding pens for slaves awaiting auction now houses the Equal Justice Initiative

(EJI), founded by attorney Bryan Stevenson to secure justice for marginalized people. The EJI may be best known for exonerating death-row clients such as Walter McMillian, whose story Stevenson tells in his memoir *Just Mercy*, but its work goes beyond challenging unfair convictions and laws. It works to achieve criminal justice reform more broadly, to share the history of racial injustice, and to help poor families who have been criminalized for their poverty. I serve there as rural development manager.

Just behind the EJI offices, facing Coosa Street, is the Legacy Museum, an EJI project that documents the connection between slavery and mass incarceration in America. Visitors there learn, among other things, how convict leasing—or selling the labor of inmates often arrested and jailed on bogus or minor charges—kept slavery alive long after the Civil War. They watch recorded interviews with modern-day inmates, including Anthony Ray Hinton, who spent twenty-eight years on death row for murders he didn't commit. His conviction was overturned in 2015 because of EJI's representation.

Nearby, the National Memorial for Peace and Justice, also created by EJI, stands as the first-ever lynching memorial in the United States. EJI has documented more than 4,400 lynchings of Black people between 1877 and 1950, including fourteen from Lowndes County. At the memorial, victims' names are etched on eight hundred six-foot steel slabs—one for each county where a lynching took place—suspended from above. At first, the slabs meet visitors at eye level. Gradually, the floor slopes downward, until visitors crane their necks to read names. By the end of the pathway through the memorial, the monuments seem to hang as high as the victims they honor once did.

Plaques along the way narrate the victims' alleged offenses:

"Drinking from a white man's well," "organizing black voters," "complaining about the recent lynching of her husband," or just "standing around" in a white neighborhood. The memorial is a powerful reminder of a not-so-distant past and a chance to pay respect to men, women, and children so horrifically robbed of dignity, compassion, and humanity.

It's a quick drive from downtown Montgomery to the Lowndes County line as our tour continues, but in many ways we could be stepping back in time. For me, it's always a homecoming. I live in Montgomery now, but my heart is in the country. It's peaceful and beautiful, with cows grazing in green pastures on gently rolling hills, and moss dripping from shade trees. I love this area despite its tortured history. I feel my ancestors in this soil, and that's what keeps bringing me here. This drive always reminds me of who I am.

We drive along Highway 80, the path of the historic march from Selma to Montgomery led by Reverend Martin Luther King Jr. in 1965 to campaign for voting rights for Black people. Most of the fifty-four-mile march passed through Lowndes County, where not a single Black person was then registered to vote, even though African Americans made up a majority of the residents. White landowners made sure of that through intimidation and force.

At the town of White Hall on Highway 80 West, we pull into the Lowndes Interpretive Center, a National Park Service site commemorating the march. Exhibits also portray aspects of sharecropper life and the infamous "Tent City" where Black families lived in the mud and muck for up to two years when white landowners evicted them for daring to register to vote after the march.

The Black Power movement was born in Lowndes County, led by Stokely Carmichael, a charismatic young field secretary for the Student Nonviolent Coordinating Committee (SNCC). Carmichael was impatient with the gentler philosophy of Rev. King. He believed electoral power was a surer way to equality than moral persuasion, and he didn't see a future with Republicans or Democrats. Democrats, after all, backed Governor Wallace.

Instead, he helped create a new party, the Lowndes County Freedom Organization. Its logo, designed by SNCC volunteers Jennifer Lawson and Courtland Cox, was a snarling black panther that would soon be familiar across America. Inspired by stories of the movement in Lowndes County, Huey Newton and Bobby Seale founded the Black Panther Party in Oakland, California, and adopted the logo as its symbol.

Lowndes County's new party didn't last, but it lived long enough to get Black candidates on the ballot and to be taken seriously by local Democrats. Armed with courage, persistence, lawsuits, and the enforcement power of the federal government, Black residents finally got to exercise their franchise. In 1970, they elected three Black candidates to public office, including the county's first Black sheriff.

The struggle didn't end there, though. Cotton was no longer king, and had become a highly mechanized crop anyway, requiring far less labor than before. The economy, built on a nearly free, unskilled workforce, stagnated. There are only two traffic lights in the whole county. Wastewater treatment ranges from inadequate to nonexistent. The same is true of internet and cable television service in parts of the county. Rural hospitals are sadly lacking. A lack of modern infrastructure left Lowndes County on the sidelines when companies looked for places to locate.

Politically, Lowndes County, like other counties in the Black Belt, never had a chance. Voting power in a place as sparsely populated as Lowndes County—about 11,000 people at last count—doesn't translate into clout beyond the county's borders. County residents still suffer from widespread poverty and neglect, even though Montgomery is just a few miles down the road.

That brings us to the present. An estimated 90 percent of Lowndes households have failing or inadequate wastewater systems, although no one took the time to count until my organization, then called the Alabama Center for Rural Enterprise (ACRE), organized a door-to-door survey. The head of one of those households for years was Pamela Rush. Pam, a forty-two-year-old mother with a cautious smile and a hint of shyness, greeted many of my tour groups at the door of the faded blue single-wide trailer she shared with her two children. Presidential candidate Bernie Sanders, as well as famous activists like Jane Fonda and Reverend Dr. William Barber of the Poor People's Campaign, traveled down the dusty road to Pam's home, where they saw a picture that was hard to shake.

The trailer barely protected Pamela and her children, now ages eleven and sixteen, from the elements. Gaps in the walls had let opossums and other wild animals from the surrounding woods squeeze in, so Pam had stuffed rags in the holes and set traps outside the front door. Visitors were cautioned to watch their step on the sloping, flimsy floors, which were soft under foot in spots.

Pam's monthly checks—less than $1,000 a month from disability and child support payments—didn't stretch far enough to cover repairs. Still, she did her best to make a comfortable home for her children, shopping secondhand at the Salvation Army. The trailer was musty, poorly ventilated, and dimly lit, with water-stained popcorn ceilings and exposed electrical wiring. But Pam had arranged an old sofa and chairs in a cozy semicircle around the television set and hung framed prints on the mildew-streaked walls. A mobile of three brown-skinned angels, bearing the words "Angels live here," hung from the wall.

In Pam's daughter's room a different kind of adornment hung from the headboard—a mask for a CPAP machine—until that room became unlivable. The child suffers from asthma and needed the machine to breathe at night amid the mold thriving in the damp walls.

At the rear of the home, overlooking a small yard and dense woods, was a collapsed deck. Beside the deck a pipe spewed raw sewage onto the ground. The toilet paper and feces told a story of the lost American dream much more clearly than Pam ever could. The pride and independence of home ownership came to rest there, in that stinking pool.

Visitors walked through Pam's house and left shaken. Everyone agreed it was unacceptable and that somebody should do something. Someone eventually did, but that comes much later in our story.

People ask sometimes why someone like Pam doesn't just move. A look at her mortgage papers provides one reason. She paid about $113,000 for the trailer in 1995, with an interest rate of 10 percent. Twenty-four years later, she still owed $13,000, but the trailer was worthless. Despite this, payments came due each month. And buying a septic system was out of the question. New ones in Lowndes, with its impermeable soils and high water tables, can easily cost more than $15,000, and nearly twice that if there is a need for an engineered system. This does not include the cost of perc tests—tests that determine whether the soil can absorb fluids—or design. We recently received bids for $21,000 and $28,000 for an engineered system on a half-acre of land.

That's an example of the structural poverty that traps good, hard-working people where they are.

This shouldn't happen in twenty-first-century America. Yet it does, and not just in Lowndes County. Poor people in rural areas around the country face similar problems. Too many Americans live without any affordable means of cleanly disposing of the waste from their toilets, and must live with the resulting filth. They lack what most Americans take for granted: the right to flush and forget.

I call it America's dirty secret, and I'm bringing it out in the open.

I came to this fight accidentally, but looking back on my life, everything pointed me this way. My parents, Mattie and J.C. Coleman, were active in the civil rights movement. Our house was a place other activists, including icons like Carmichael, would visit to talk about strategy and issues of the day. I loved those front-porch conversations, and I soaked them all up. Maybe organizing is in my blood, because I've been fighting for what's right since high school, when my father and I campaigned successfully for the removal of a principal and superintendent who were racist and substandard.

I went to college, got married, joined the Air Force, taught school in Washington, DC, North Carolina, and Detroit, worked in a congressional office, and got my master's degree in history. Yet my roots kept pulling me back. I had strong family ties that stretched back over generations. My parents were still here, and so were my ancestors. Go to any cemetery in this county and you'll see the graves of my people. I sense their blood and sweat in this fertile soil.

I'm still a country girl at heart. I grew up living close to this land, raised on homegrown food and steeped in country values. Nobody had much, but everyone shared. You didn't visit someone without being pressed to take something they'd grown, cooked, or made. We were in tune with nature in ways most city people will never understand. I wanted my young daughter to look at the night sky and see stars away from the glare of city lights. And I wanted to help hard-working people who hadn't had my opportunities.

So in 2001, I became a consultant in economic development for Lowndes County, and it didn't take long to realize the challenges I was up against. We needed jobs, but companies weren't eager to invest in places without infrastructure, where they would have to spend their own money on improvements that the local tax base could never afford, unless the companies were looking to locate something nobody else wanted, like a landfill. At first, I was focused on business and didn't realize how many households lacked the most basic plumbing. Then a convergence of events changed the trajectory of my life.

I'd been looking for outside help for our county, and I found it in Bob Woodson, the conservative founder of the National Center for Neighborhood Enterprise, now called the Woodson Center. I had met Bob years before in Tuscaloosa, Alabama, at Stillman College, where he spoke at the 21st Century Youth Leadership Camp. I had taken students there from the school where I taught in Washington, DC.

Woodson was a MacArthur "Genius" grant recipient and an expert on urban issues. He advocated for public-private partnerships connecting community leaders and organizations with training and funding to uplift their neighborhoods. While I didn't disagree with his approach, I did take issue with some of the politics associated with it, and during our first meeting I let him know—it seemed to me that he disregarded history and expected people to pull themselves up by their bootstraps when they had no boots to begin with.

Then, after the presidential election of 2000 ended controversially, I saw Woodson on television speaking on behalf of the Bush campaign. I don't know why, but somehow I knew he was going to help me. First, though, I had to reach him.

I found out he was scheduled to speak in Washington, DC, and I scraped up enough money to go. At the summit, I waited for Woodson to finish speaking, and I followed him when he left the stage. He stopped and listened to me as I described the challenges of economic development work in Lowndes County. I told him that we were between Selma and Montgomery, where throngs of well-meaning people passed each year to commemorate Dr. King's march. Yet along the route, folks were still living in third-world conditions, and nobody was fighting for them. I described how hard it was to draw attention to the problems of poor rural communities. He said he was an urban guy, accustomed to finding solutions for the challenges of urban poverty, but he would be interested in learning more. Eventually, he agreed to come to Lowndes County, where he would surely get that education.

I had some sites mapped out for Woodson's visit when I got a call from Marzette Wright, a county commissioner. She said there was a family out in the county that I needed to see. They'd been written about recently in the daily newspaper *Montgomery Advertiser* because they had a terrible problem. Their septic system wasn't working, and they'd been threatened with eviction and arrest because of the raw sewage flowing from their home. The cost of fixing it was far beyond what they could ever afford. I added them to the route.

I grew up poor in the 1960s, when people in our community still used outhouses. At night, we used "slop jars" so we didn't have to go outdoors to relieve ourselves. In the morning, we'd empty the jars in the woods or an outhouse. Even so, I wasn't prepared for what we would see on our tour. I didn't yet fully grasp how little things had changed in Lowndes County since I'd been gone, or that in some ways they were worse.

But I was about to find out as our caravan of cars pulled off the main road and headed toward the home of Mattie and Odell McMeans.

The McMeanses were a middle-aged couple with a large family. They lived in a sort of compound of five white trailers with a small country church nearby. Eighteen family members lived there at the time. The homes sat on an incline, and as we approached, we were shocked to see raw sewage streaming alongside the sloping road.

We had barely parked our van near the houses when the pastor from the little church came to greet us. He was crying. He'd been notified his congregation could no longer worship in the building, which had no septic tank. Sewage was straight-piped outdoors from the church. Not only did the pastor have to suspend church services, but he had also been threatened with arrest if he didn't fix the problem. In Alabama, failure to maintain a permitted septic tank is a criminal misdemeanor.

It was heartbreaking.

The McMeans family did have a septic tank, but it was broken. Like the pastor, they'd been ordered to rectify the situation. And like the pastor, Mr. McMeans cried because he couldn't come up with the money.

We left Mr. McMeans and the pastor and went to the courthouse to see the judge who oversaw the case. She agreed there was a better way to handle it and said she'd try to help, which she ultimately did. After the *Montgomery Advertiser* article, donations began pouring in. The McMeans family was out of immediate jeopardy.

Meanwhile, though, a firestorm was brewing. In all his work with urban poverty, Bob had never seen anything like what he saw that day, and he was horrified. Well connected in Washington, he took action. He called *Washington Post* journalist

William Raspberry, and he must have made a compelling case. Raspberry wrote powerfully about the criminalization of Lowndes's poor people in his syndicated column on March 18, 2002. He quoted Woodson:

It just blew my mind. . . . People living without sewers or septic tanks, with waste running off into an open ditch. A third of the residents living in trailers, which start losing value the day they buy them, because they can get loans for trailers but not for houses on land they own. Kids attending ramshackle schools with coal-fired furnaces and as many as a third of them spending time out of school with respiratory illnesses. . . . I've just talked to a man whose 90-something-year-old father is about to be evicted from a place he owns because he doesn't have a septic tank. It will cost the county more to take care of him after his eviction than it would cost to put in a septic tank for him.

Woodson called the problem a failure of the civil rights movement. I disagreed. I saw it as a failure of government to address the needs of the rural poor, another chapter in a long history of the marginalization of poor minorities and rural residents. While my theory differed from Woodson's diagnosis, I appreciated his concern and his effort. And I agreed with him on one important point.

"We need to declare what's happening in Lowndes County a 'virtual hurricane,'" he told Raspberry. "You know what would happen if a real hurricane struck the area and wiped everything out. We would go in with engineers, builders, truckloads of septic tanks. The government, volunteers and the private sector would all come together to do what needed to be done."

The column got the kind of media attention that rural communities seldom see. It marked the first time the county's sewage situation made the national news, and the story didn't stop with the *Washington Post*. I called the Associated Press to report the story, and the story of people in Alabama being arrested because they couldn't afford septic tanks went out on the news wires across the country.

The story was assigned to a reporter who wrote, "Human waste dumped outside of trailers and houses can become breeding grounds for everything from diphtheria to cholera, health officials said." At long last, this caught Washington's attention. But nothing moves fast in DC, and the squeaky wheel usually gets the grease. It's taken us years to be squeaky enough, but we're finally getting there.

Maybe because of my parents' example, I can't just stand by and watch an injustice. After that visit to the McMeans home in 2002, I knew I had a new fight on my hands. I stayed in Alabama, working for Woodson and the National Center for Neighborhood Enterprise for several years as a consultant in rural development. I founded the Alabama Center for Rural Enterprise (ACRE), which has evolved into the Center for Rural Enterprise and Environmental Justice (CREEJ). Our mission is to reduce health, economic, and environmental disparities and improve access to clean air, water, and soil in marginalized rural communities. We aim to influence policy, inspire innovation, drive research, and amplify the voices of community leaders, all within the context of a changing climate.

My team organized community meetings and door-to-door surveys that confirmed the McMeans family's situation was far from unique. We secured funding for septic systems for those in need and even donations of new homes. I published articles, conducted media interviews, and spoke everywhere I could to keep the issue alive. We pressured state officials to stop criminalizing poverty by threatening people with arrest for failing to maintain working septic systems. Eventually, they backed off.

Despite all that, by 2014, Lowndes County still hadn't achieved the "virtual hurricane status" that Woodson spoke of and Raspberry wrote about. However, another community did. Flint, Michigan's urban water crisis captivated the country's attention and our lawmakers' intentions when the news hit that Flint's children were drinking water contaminated by lead. Once the people in power there finally admitted the problem, they were forced to take strong action. It was a crisis of major proportions, and there was no ignoring it.

Flint gained attention because infrastructure failed. In places like Lowndes County, however, there's no infrastructure in the first place. But in Lowndes County, as in Flint, a public health crisis has emerged. It's arrived in the form of hookworms.

Although hookworms aren't fatal, they can slow physical and mental development in children, lead to intestinal diseases, and cause various other forms of misery, from fatigue to abdominal pain and diarrhea. Researchers are just starting to look into how far they might have spread across the Black Belt. But the hookworms might have evaded discovery completely if not for a chance happening one day.

I had made the mistake of wearing a dress to visit a family with a hole in the ground full of raw sewage in their yard. Mosquitoes were out in force, and my legs were soon covered with bites. Later, I developed a mysterious rash. When doctors couldn't diagnose it, I began to wonder if third-world conditions might be bringing third-world diseases to our region.

I contacted Dr. Peter Hotez, a renowned tropical disease specialist and founding dean of the National School of Tropical Medicine at the Baylor College of Medicine in Houston, to see if he'd be interested in investigating whether that might be true. He and his team came through for us with a peer-reviewed study. In a sample of fifty-five adults and children, 34.5 percent tested positive for hookworms. Now we are preparing to expand our studies seeking evidence of soil-transmitted helminths—parasitic intestinal worms—to other areas. It's very likely that we'll find that raw sewage is the cause not only of hookworm's return but also of other tropical diseases right here on American soil.

Ever since news of the hookworm infestation broke in 2017, public interest has surged. I've testified before a United Nations panel in Geneva, Switzerland. I've even consulted with members of Congress about legislation to fund a nationwide study of wastewater treatment. We want to know how widespread the problem is, and we want solutions—including new, affordable technology. Three senators, Cory Booker (D-NJ), Doug Jones (D-AL), and Shelley Moore Capito (R-WV), have introduced bills to address the issue in a comprehensive way. New legislation also authored by Booker, called the Study, Treat, Observe, and Prevent (STOP) Neglected Diseases of Poverty Act, aims to assess the extent of conditions such as hookworm infestation, educate health care providers, and fund research into treatments.

Meanwhile, poor people wait.

The situation should shock the conscience of all Americans. It certainly made an impression on Philip Alston, the United Nations special rapporteur on extreme poverty and human rights, when I took him on a Lowndes County tour in late 2017. Here's how he described it later:

In Alabama, I saw various houses in rural areas that were surrounded by cesspools of sewage that flowed out of broken or non-existent septic systems. The State Health Department had no idea of how many households exist in these conditions, despite the grave health consequences. Nor did they have any plan to find out or devise a plan to do something about it. But since the great majority of White folks live in the cities, which are well served by government built and maintained sewerage systems, and most of the rural folks in areas like Lowndes County are Black, the problem doesn't appear on the political or governmental radar screen.

I used to think this was just a problem of the Black Belt. Here, those who have septic systems find they're prone to failure because of the high clay content of our soil. Septic systems are designed for solids to sink to the bottom of tanks while liquids are released to drain into the surrounding earth. But clay holds water rather than letting it drain. Tanks fill quickly, and overwhelmed systems back up and break down.

But ours isn't the only soil that doesn't absorb wastewater. I started to understand this one day when I took a documentary film crew to a mobile home in Lowndes County where sewage drained from a pipe and into the yard. Normally, people are shocked when I lead these tours, but on this trip, the young white filmmaker seemed unfazed. "I've seen this before," she whispered. "Was it in other rural southern towns of mostly poor Black residents like this one?" I asked. No, she said. It was at her grandmother's house in rural Southern Illinois.

As my travels expanded along with my environmental

justice work, I began hearing about, and then seeing, the same problem in places from rural white Kentucky to unincorporated Latinx neighborhoods in California to Native American reservations in the West. It plagues people in Alaska and Hawaii. It happens mostly in the country, where people live beyond the reach of city utilities. But country people aren't the only Americans living alongside raw sewage. I recently visited Centreville, Illinois, a small, impoverished city in the Greater St. Louis area. It's a mostly Black community where untreated waste streamed alongside homes even though residents pay for municipal wastewater service. Unjust as it may seem, it's not unusual for residents of poor and marginalized communities to be forced to pay for infrastructure that doesn't work.

Nationwide, the problem has been ignored by policymakers on all levels. Local, state, and federal governments fail to invest in rural infrastructure. They fail to protect poor consumers from buying and installing shoddy equipment pitched by unscrupulous contractors. And they fail to encourage the development of new technology that might provide long-term, affordable solutions.

Now it's becoming too big a problem to ignore. Climate change, with its rising sea levels and heavy rains that saturate soil, threatens to bring sewage to more backyards, and not only those of poor minorities. In Florida, for example, a study found that 64 percent of Miami-Dade County septic systems could malfunction by 2040, threatening water supplies.

It's a crisis that deserves the attention it's finally getting. That's where I come in. I've been called the "Erin Brockovich of Sewage" and the "Empress of Effluent," titles I never aspired to but I'll gladly accept if it helps.

I want to show as many people as I can what this crisis looks like, feels like, and smells like. I want you to meet the people who live with this every day and to see what scores of people—politicians, journalists, health officials, activists, students, industry executives, billionaire philanthropists, celebrities, and filmmakers—have seen on my tours. And I want to show you how we—and I—got to this point.

We'll start in Lowndes County, once again Ground Zero for a movement.

Chapter 2

I was born in Birmingham and lived for a time in Montgomery, but my parents wanted to raise their family in the country. My father was from an unincorporated area called Gordonsville in Lowndes County, and in 1968, when I was ten, we settled nearby in the tiny community of Blackbelt. My parents, my three brothers, my sister, and I lived in a concrete block house with a big yard in a neighborhood full of poor families with big dreams and lots of faith.

We children had to be creative and industrious. When the boys decided that it was time to have a basketball court, they went into the woods and cut trees for the post. Pool was a favorite pastime, so one of the neighborhood kids made a miniature pool table from a NeHi soft-drink crate, and somebody brought marbles to use for balls. That pool table provided endless hours of fun.

Even in 1968, indoor plumbing was a luxury. Most families had outhouses. For water, neighborhood children would walk to Miss Nell's house with buckets to use her hand-operated pump. It was time-consuming, but the water was so cold and delicious that it seemed worth it. We had an electric pump at home—I guess there were degrees of poverty—but I enjoyed the ritual at Miss Nell's anyway. It felt good to carry water home after I'd pumped it up from the earth.

In the evenings we'd sit on Miss Shug's front porch and listen to the latest R&B music from Ernie's Record Mart on WLAC radio out of Nashville. If you grew up in the South when I did, you know the importance of front porches. That's where people would gather to catch up on gossip, swap stories, and share news. In the days before air conditioning, it was cooler on the porch in the evenings, and children could listen to music or play in the yard while grown-ups talked. Most people had big families then—I was the oldest of five children—so there was plenty of company.

Miss Shug was still young then. She was a beautiful woman and hip for her time—I remember her wearing jumpsuits, which are back in fashion today. She was not only a community mother to us all, but also an activist. She'd tell stories of mass meetings and organizing and getting out the vote. She talked about the social and savings clubs that I later realized were the foundation from which the original Black Panther Party grew in Lowndes County. Years later, she'd play a big role in bringing me back home to Alabama.

Friends were always stopping by to visit my parents, including people from the "Movement." I heard names like Dennis Banks, Russell Means, and Kwame Nkrumah. I met people like Bob Mants, John Jackson, Willie "Mukasa" Ricks, and Stokely Carmichael. They were people who were working across the globe toward a new vision of justice. At the time, I did not realize I was not among common men. I learned about the Student Nonviolent Coordinating Committee (SNCC) and the Southern Christian Leadership Conference (SCLC). And most of all, I learned about serving my community for the greater good.

My parents functioned much in the same way as jailhouse

lawyers: people came to them for help, maybe because they'd lived other places. My father gave sound advice, and my mother drafted letters, interpreted government correspondence, filled out applications, and even did taxes. When the courts ruled that the school district had to educate special needs children, my mother became the trusted person who could convince parents it was okay to send the children to school. The school district hired her, she drove a bus, and she was also a teacher's aide.

My parents exposed us as best they could to things not everyone in our neighborhood commonly knew about. When I'd meet people who were white and educated, sometimes they were surprised by what I knew. I didn't realize it at the time, but my parents were giving me the foundation to find common ground with all kinds of people. I still remember how my father's love of big-band music helped me make conversation at my first Washington, DC, cocktail party.

Both my parents grew up in the Jim Crow era, when Black people in the South survived by keeping their heads down and never complaining no matter how bad things were. But times were changing. My father was especially affected by the lynching of Emmett Till, the fourteen-year-old Chicago boy who was beaten, mutilated, shot, and dumped in the Tallahatchie River for allegedly flirting with a white woman while he was visiting relatives in Mississippi in 1955. My father resolved that he would not live his life in subservience. He became even more determined after serving in the military and seeing more of the world that he was not going to be denied freedom when he returned.

The conversations I heard at home helped me put together pieces of things that had been worrying me. Growing up in the sixties, especially in the places we lived, meant living with upheaval. In 1963, we were living in Birmingham, where my father worked for Hayes Aircraft. I remember the teenagers in my community going to jail for demonstrating. My mother even demonstrated. I felt the tension in the air before my five-year-old mind could understand it.

On November 22, 1963, my father came home from work and told my mother, "They finally got him," before beginning to cry. He was talking about President John F. Kennedy, who was assassinated that day. Later, he talked of moving the family to England, where he had served during the Korean War. We watched the funeral on TV, and it seemed to last for days. I still remember little John John saluting his father's casket. Little did I know the role the Kennedys would indirectly play in my life.

On April 4, 1968, my mother returned from work earlier than usual. Dr. Martin Luther King Jr. had been shot, and businesses were closing for fear of rioting. By then we were living in Montgomery, where my father worked at Maxwell Air Force Base. The ever-present tension thickened. The next day in school, the principal played Mahalia Jackson's song "Precious Lord" over the intercom, and I started to cry. A classmate and I hugged each other. We had not been close friends before that day, but we shared the pain of something we did not quite understand.

My father always listened to the news. At five in the evening, the entire family would sit in front of the television, glued to *The Huntley-Brinkley Report*, the nightly NBC news program. The local news would broadcast the names of soldiers who had died in Vietnam. Breaking news bulletins were common. One of those bulletins announced another assassination, this time of Robert Kennedy. Again, the tension hung heavy in the air.

I began to wonder what I could do to help bring peace and brotherhood to the world. I started writing songs and poetry. If the world was not the way it was supposed to be, maybe I could make it so in my writing. I read voraciously, hungry to learn about the rest of the world and places I had never seen.

Race was not something I thought of much when I was younger. Blacks and whites lived separately, and that was the way it was. But things were changing. It was a time of firsts for Black people. Muhammad Ali refused to go to Vietnam in protest as a conscientious objector, and the Ali–Frazier fight was a big deal in my house. We would crowd around the television to see Black actors in starring roles, which were slowly increasing. From *Julia*, starring Diahann Carroll, to *The Flip Wilson Show*, TV was starting to provide glimpses of different ways life could unfold for us.

The Jackson Five were all close to my age, and they represented infinite possibilities. I wrote a song called "You Got to Have Soul" and sent it to an address in an ad in my mother's *True Story* magazines. They sent me a contract, and I dreamed of promoting my music on *The Tonight Show* with Johnny Carson. Later, I realized they probably sent everyone a contract along with a bill to make the song into a record.

I would walk along the red dirt roads or between rows of cornstalks and marvel at the splendor around me. I imagined building my own community, complete with a church, school, and hospital. In the summer I'd pick plums and blackberries or break off an ear of corn from a stalk, sinking my teeth into its sweet milk. You could say I grew up close to nature, but we didn't call it that. It was just our world.

I guess I knew I was different when I couldn't cook like other girls. I made biscuits so hard the dogs rejected them. I was no better at sewing. I couldn't understand why I had to take home economics when it wouldn't help me get into college. Then life started opening up to me in unexpected ways.

• • •

One day, a group of people came to visit my parents in Black-belt. The group included Norman Lumpkin, a Montgomery television news reporter, Sue Thompson of the American Civil Liberties Union, and a reporter and crew from the British Broadcasting Company (BBC) in London. They were visiting because my mother had been sterilized at John A. Andrew Hospital in Tuskegee after she gave birth to her fifth child, my little brother.

Apparently, many poor pregnant women were coerced into submitting to sterilization before the hospital's physicians would deliver their babies. This became a public concern when it came to light that two Black teenagers, the Relf sisters, were sterilized because they were deemed mentally incompetent and thus unfit to be parents in the future. The Southern Poverty Law Center filed a lawsuit, and my mother became a spokesperson for these women in rural communities. It was the second time Tuskegee was associated with unethical medical practices toward poor African Americans. Tuskegee was also the location of the infamous syphilis experiment, a forty-year study in which Black men with syphilis were neither told their diagnosis nor treated while researchers observed the long-term effects of the disease.

The afternoon of the interview, our entire family was seated in the front yard with the BBC reporter. My mother mentioned that I wrote poems, and Norman Lumpkin asked to see them. I gladly brought him stacks to read. He said that he was going to tell his friend Tracy Larkin about me. At that time, Tracy hosted a weekly television show on WSFA in Montgomery called *Focus*. Shortly after that, I was invited to recite my poetry on Tracy's show, and I began appearing regularly. I was in the tenth grade.

My parents continued to be active in the community. My father even ran for sheriff against an incumbent he'd supported in the past. John Hulett was a leader in the struggle for voter registration in Lowndes County, and in 1970 he became the county's first Black sheriff. Hulett had received many death threats while he was running, and my father personally guarded him. But after his election, Hulett began cutting back-room deals with white power brokers and building a political machine. Believing Hulett had turned his back on his people, my father declared his own candidacy for sheriff. He lost the election, but not his standing in the community.

My mother was active in the National Welfare Rights Association, among other things. Our home was a stopover for many students and civil rights activists who came to visit my parents from around the country. This only fed my hunger to become a force for change.

I was beginning to realize how substandard my education was. After an appearance on *Focus*, I was asked to write an article for a newsletter. I wrote about my high school, Lowndes County Training School, where I was a junior. The resulting uproar changed my life.

Lowndes County Training School had been the Black school during segregation. In those days, white school boards typically named Black high schools "training schools," a degrading term. The school system was still mostly Black because once white parents saw that integration was unavoidable, they enrolled their children in newly created private "academies." The principal of my school was Dr. Robert R. Pierce, a Black man who'd achieved popularity among white people for openly opposing the civil rights movement. It was alleged that he had fired a weapon into the house of a local Black activist while riding with the Ku Klux Klan. Movement leaders had campaigned to have him removed as principal in the 1960s, to no avail.

He received little supervision from the white school super-intendent or the state. The education of Black children was not a priority. He had also been accused of supplying young Black girls from Lowndes County to white men in Montgomery and the surrounding area for sex. When a nine-year-old Black girl was found dead in Montgomery with a pajama bottom wrapped around her neck, rumors swirled that Dr. Pierce was involved, but he was never charged.

In my article, I told how classes stopped at our school around midday. After lunch, Pierce threw dance parties. Students who didn't go to the dances would find other ways to occupy their time, as teenagers will. Once, Pierce sponsored a showing of *The Mack*, an R-rated blaxploitation movie about an Oakland pimp, at the high school during school hours. Students from seventh through twelfth grades paid two dollars each to view the movie.

That part of the article grabbed the attention of the people from the American Friends Service Committee. I received a call from Freddie Fox of the AFSC. He was the founder of the Alabama Students for Civil Rights and a senior fellow at the Robert F. Kennedy Memorial Foundation. He came to meet with my parents and me, and brought Jack Guillebeaux, director of the Montgomery office of AFSC. I gave them details.

The afternoon that Freddie and Jack visited my school, a dance was going on, and most students were headed there. The halls were so crowded that school officials had no idea Freddie and Jack were in the middle of the chaos. The students who opted to stay in class mainly just sat talking to friends or to the teachers, who tried to make the best of a bad situation. Freddie and Jack came away even more determined to take action. They instructed me on Alabama school law, showing me how to document infractions in a small notebook that I guarded carefully. I filled pages rapidly.

My parents, along with Reverend Arthur Lee Knight and his family, started Concerned Parents and Students for Quality Education in Lowndes County. Arlinda Knight and I were the only two student members of the organization, and we became vastly unpopular. Our peers felt that we were disrupting their good times. They had no idea that a worthless education could disrupt their lives forever.

The backlash at school grew dangerous. The Concerned Parents group held public meetings, and one time several high school students attended. Our guest was an army recruiter who talked about how graduates of our school had trouble meeting requirements to enter the armed services. Then it was my turn to speak. I said that it was time to end ignorance, that ignorant parents have ignorant children, and I did not want my children to be ignorant. The students in attendance were outraged. They misinterpreted what I said to mean that they were ignorant and their offspring would be as well.

The next day in class I heard a commotion in the hallway. A crowd of students had surrounded Arlinda Knight, and some were hitting her. I was called to the office over the intercom and told to leave the high school and go to the office of the elementary school principal. When I arrived, a distraught Arlinda was already there. I called my father, and he said to stay there while he located Arlinda's father.

We were petrified. This was the first time either of us had feared for our safety. We were sent to wait in the classroom of Mrs. Sarah Logan, who was not only a relative of mine, but had served as an original member of the Lowndes County Freedom Party. When she and another teacher, Dorothy Hinson, were fired for their participation in civil rights work, they became plaintiffs in a landmark case against the state. They won when an appeals court found that the Alabama legislature had given

Black Belt counties special exemptions from the state's tenure laws so they could fire Black teachers at will.

While we waited, Rev. Knight and my father rushed to the high school and went directly to Pierce's office. According to my father, Rev. Knight closed the door and my father placed a gun to Pierce's head and demanded to see us. If there was a scratch on either of us, he said, Pierce was dead.

Pierce called for Arlinda and me to come to his office, and also called the sheriff's office, not knowing authorities were already on their way because my father had alerted them. Everybody knew my father was a veteran and almost always carried a gun. He knew the history of Lowndes County and why it was called "Bloody Lowndes," and he had received death threats at times. Some people even called him the "high sheriff."

When a deputy arrived at the school, Dr. Pierce asked him to arrest my father because he had pointed a gun at him. Rev. Knight said he was present and did not see anything. Arlinda and I arrived, escorted by the elementary school principal. When we entered the office, our fathers hugged us and asked if were harmed in any way. We both said we were okay. Dr. Pierce looked scared. He said nothing. The deputy told us not to hesitate to call if we felt threatened. He also told Dr. Pierce he was going to hold him responsible for our safety.

In the meantime, a few girls told a sheriff's deputy that some young men had left school to get guns and planned to shoot us. The deputy rounded up the young men and warned them to stay away from us or go to jail. His warning must have hit home because we had no more problems.

Concerned Parents and Students took our allegations to the Lowndes County School Board, and three of the five school members voted to suspend Pierce. That set off a ripple effect throughout the school. An acting principal took charge. Teachers who had skated for years now attempted to teach. Others who'd been unhappy with the chaos felt newly empowered to speak.

My activism got attention. I was still a regular on *Focus*, and the *Montgomery Advertiser* covered our story. Through Alabama Students for Civil Rights, I formed alliances with activists in other parts of the state. The Robert F. Kennedy Memorial Foundation took notice of my work as well and invited me to become a Robert Kennedy youth fellow. They sponsored my first trip to Washington, DC, where I was invited to attend the National Education Association's Conference on Educational Neglect.

On the trip, I was joined by Freddie Fox, Joseph Battle, and Nim Russell. Joseph and Nim were high school students in Russell County, Alabama, where Joseph's mom was a community activist, and Nim was vice president of the Alabama Students for Civil Rights chapter. Our escort in Washington was Michael Hughes, a senior fellow at the RFK Memorial. Michael was a Hopi-Sioux Indian. It was shortly after the Wounded Knee takeover, and I was fascinated as Michael told us about the American Indian Movement and the plight of Native Americans on reservations.

Our Washington schedule included tours of the usual sites, such as the Lincoln and Jefferson memorials and the Washington Monument, and attending the conference. Jesse Jackson's speech was a highlight for me that I would recall often once I became a teacher. He said, "Teachers are called to teach, like preachers are called to preach." Other than Jackson, I found the conference disappointing. Speakers seemed to be whitewashing concerns instead of applying practical solutions to pressing problems. They were wasting time while the clock was running out on my education. I made my feelings known when I got a chance to speak. A small delegation from the

National Education Association came to us and tried to appease us, promising support for our efforts in Alabama. I took a wait-and-see attitude.

We visited the Memorial Foundation's offices in an elegant Georgetown townhouse and discussed student rights with some of Robert Kennedy's old friends and allies. We learned about landmark Supreme Court decisions that guaranteed our rights to free expression and due process. And then we attended a reception at the tony Chevy Chase, Maryland, home of David Hackett, one of Robert Kennedy's closest friends dating back to childhood. Now he was executive director of the foundation. David was the inspiration for the character Phineas in John Knowles's coming-of-age novel *A Separate Peace*, the good-hearted prep-school boy who excelled in everything he tried. David also shared Robert Kennedy's passion for justice.

I later learned that most of the people at the reception were board members of the Memorial. One white couple, the Hacketts, struck up a conversation with me and asked me about my fight in Lowndes County. They asked if I had a wish, and what it would be. I told them that I wanted to leave Lowndes County and go to boarding school. I knew the education I'd been getting wasn't enough for me to be accepted to an Ivy League university. Adults I knew had told me about feeling unprepared when they got to college, and I wanted to be ready.

We left Washington feeling good because we felt we had friends in other places who were looking out for us. I didn't know it yet, but I'd be back soon.

Back in Alabama, Dr. Pierce, the suspended principal, was not giving up without a fight. The Black teachers association filed a federal lawsuit on Pierce's behalf, and I had to get ready for my deposition. I met with our attorney, Howard Mandell, in the Montgomery office of the AFSC. This was my first time being questioned by an attorney under oath, and Howard was concerned I'd come across like a young Angela Davis, a prominent and controversial activist.

It was nerve-wracking as Howard prepared Arlinda and me for the questions we might face. Arlinda had accused Dr. Pierce of touching her inappropriately, and she knew Pierce's attorneys would try to disparage her character. This was not her family's first time facing intense pressure. Arlinda's father was a native of Lowndes County. Like many people before him, he had moved to Michigan during the Great Migration, escaping the Jim Crow South and pursuing economic opportunity. Later, he and his wife and four children became the first Black family to move into Dearborn, Michigan, a suburb of Detroit. However, the violence and intimidation were so great that Rev. Knight moved his family back to Detroit and later to Lowndes County, where they owned property.

The depositions went well, and the next major showdown was at a meeting of the Board of Education in Lowndes County. Pierce was there with his lawyers and Joe Reed, a representative of the teachers association. Howard and the board had ample information about Pierce's abuse of authority. The most damaging evidence would come from the many female students who were prepared to share details of his sexual advances toward them. Before the hearing began, Pierce resigned and the lawsuit was dropped. Reed sent word to us that he had represented Pierce only because his job required it.

Pierce had ruled over Lowndes County Training School for forty years. His reign was finally over, and we rejoiced.

The summer of 1975 was filled with excitement for me, as I was going to Washington to study the workings of Capitol Hill as a Robert Kennedy youth fellow. I'd be living in Chevy Chase with the Hackett family. David and Judith Hackett lived with their five children in a large, two-story, white stucco home at the top of a steep driveway in a wealthy neighborhood. It was a different world for me. In Washington, people seemed to walk faster than they did in Alabama. In fact, everything moved faster. And I saw women doing jobs that were only performed by men in Montgomery and Lowndes County—driving trucks, working on telephone poles, and patrolling as police officers.

I attended Bethesda-Chevy Chase High School (BCC)— which was considered one of the top public high schools in the United States—for a course in English as a second language. This class was chosen for me because I sometimes spoke in southern dialect, and I guess I sounded vastly different from my upper-crust Massachusetts-elite hosts. I was convinced the class was necessary for me to be able to get into a good college, so I didn't feel belittled. The teacher said I didn't need it, but I enjoyed getting to know my classmates, who were the children of diplomats. I was the only Black student in the class, and the only child whose native tongue was English.

Mrs. Hackett was a former ballerina with the London Royal Ballet and still had a British accent. She accompanied me to school on my first day, and when she introduced herself to my teacher, she said I was her daughter. As a child of the civil rights movement in Alabama, I was ready for my international classmates to snicker, but they didn't. They actually seemed to believe her. Sometimes Victoria, the Hacketts' youngest daughter, would tell people that I was her sister. Through the Hacketts, I was beginning to see the meaning of Dr. King's dream of a time when people would be judged on the content of their character and not the color of their skin.

On weekdays, I'd take the bus to school. The only Black people I saw on the way were maids. Mrs. Hackett told me that one Black family, from South Africa, lived in the community, but I never saw them. After class, I liked to look at the beautiful homes and buildings, including the National Cathedral. It was so different from the red dirt and dusty roads of Lowndes County. I used to imagine living in DC as an adult. I found it intriguing that I could look at people without immediately knowing their race or nationality. Spending time in such a cosmopolitan city gave me a new sense of the world.

The Memorial Foundation was on 30th Street, just off M Street, among the beautiful row houses. Former members of the Kennedy administration visited regularly. I made friends with another intern, Emily Rosen, who came from a wealthy family in Shaker Heights, Ohio. Together, we visited the Capitol several times a week, but one time stands out as the most memorable.

Emily and I had developed a proposal for a summer internship project for high school students to serve in the Capitol, and we met with Senator Edward Kennedy in his office to discuss it. It was a special occasion, and we marked it by trading our usual jeans and T-shirts for dresses. We waited nervously in a waiting area until we were escorted into the senator's office. I had never met a United States senator before, and I'd never met a Kennedy in person.

Sen. Kennedy quickly put us at ease. Instead of the usual awards, his office walls featured his children's drawings as well as some pictures addressed to "Uncle Ted." Looking directly at me and addressing me by name, he told me that he'd heard about my work in Lowndes County, and applauded my quest for a quality education. He also complimented Emily's work in photography. But mostly we talked about our proposal. He said he preferred giving internships to college students, not high school students, but we were pleased that he at least listened respectfully to our ideas.

The Hacketts often held dinner parties, where I met lobbyists, activists, politicians, and visitors from other countries. On some hot evenings, Mr. Hackett would take the family and me swimming at Ethel Kennedy's home in McLean, Virginia. I was fascinated by the size of the house, and a little star-struck too.

Mr. Hackett assigned reading material for all of his children during the summer. I remember that Bobby, the Hacketts' youngest son, was reading Plato's *Republic*. The children were expected to discuss what they read with their father, and to list words they didn't know and look up and then write out the definitions. Mr. Hackett also encouraged my writing, taking time from his busy schedule to read what I wrote, ask engaging questions, and edit my work.

One day I arrived at the Memorial as usual, and he asked if I'd like to attend Milton Academy in Massachusetts, his alma mater. I had shared with him my desire to attend Radcliffe College and Harvard Law School. My goal was to be the first Black female Supreme Court justice. Mr. Hackett said I would need to attend a good high school to get into a good college, and a good college to get into a good law school. He said that at Milton, I would live at the school during the week, and on weekends I would stay either with his mother or with Marian Wright Edelman on Martha's Vineyard. Edelman was the first Black woman to be admitted to the Mississippi Bar, and she had founded the Children's Defense Fund. Dave said I would meet people from around the world. I asked whether there were any Black children at the school. He said that he didn't know, but he wanted me to talk to the headmaster, who was Black.

The only problem was that I hadn't taken any foreign language classes and would have to return to the eleventh grade to earn two years of language credits. I'd also have to start preparing for the SAT, something I'd never heard of. The counselor at my high school had never told me about college entrance exams.

Excited, I called my parents. They didn't like the idea, especially the part about repeating the eleventh grade. My parents were accustomed to me being on the honor roll and wanted me to graduate on time. They did not see the benefits and didn't know about Marian Wright Edelman.

Mr. Hackett recommended people I could call who could talk to my parents about the benefits of Milton. I called Kenneth Gibson, who had served in the army with my father and in 1970 became the first Black mayor of Newark, New Jersey. He was the one person who thought I should go to Milton Academy. Others disagreed. Freddie Fox said that people were trying to "de-niggerize" me. He always used words like that. I am certain he said the same thing to my parents.

I called Hank Sanders, an attorney and civil rights activist in Selma who'd gone to Harvard Law School after attending a Black college. Like Freddie, he disagreed that I needed to go to Milton. With Freddie and Hank on their side, I knew my parents would harden their stance. They soon began insisting that I return home.

Not wanting to concede defeat, David offered another plan. I could go to Sidwell Friends School in Washington, DC, and live with his family. By this time, however, I knew my parents wouldn't agree.

I wanted to leave Lowndes County Training School. Whenever I would state my school's name, people assumed I was in a school for bad children. The name had always carried a stigma in the South, where Black kids attended training schools, while white children went to high schools. But I had to return.

Before I left, I got to see another side of Washington. A fellow intern, Linda, had had a few encounters with the law and came from a dysfunctional family. She was enrolled in a program to finish high school. Others at the Memorial worried about my spending time with her, but she never tried to persuade me to do anything wrong. She did explain to me the lure of the streets. She also introduced me to local members of the Black Panther Party. I would frequent their office and buy literature.

One day while venturing down H Street in the Panthers' neighborhood, I decided to get my hair cut. H Street had been one of the sites of rioting in DC after the King assassination in 1968, and still held the skeletons of burned-out buildings. I found a Black barbershop and asked them to cut my hair into a short natural. I liked it and thought it fit my increasingly militant beliefs.

I was still writing poetry, and on the cover of one of my collections I drew a picture of Jesus in an afro with a Bible in his right hand and a gun in his left. I was a native of the place that gave the world the original Black Panther Party, and Stokely Carmichael always talked about Jesus coming with a sword. When Mr. Hackett saw the picture, he wasn't pleased. He didn't say much, but later that year he sent me to a workshop on nonviolence at the Martin Luther King Jr. Center for Nonviolent Social Change in Atlanta.

My summer in Washington, DC, came to an end in August, and I returned to the dusty roads and red clay dirt of Lowndes County to begin my senior year of high school. I felt empowered, and I had a plan: I was going to remove Hulda Coleman, the superintendent of schools, and change the name of my high school before I graduated.

My parents didn't recognize me at first when I got off the plane. Besides my new hairstyle, I guess I exuded a new confidence. I must have moved like someone on a mission. I was still a teenager, turning seventeen in a few days, and thinking of prom, graduation, and boys. But I had seen the possibilities that the world held, and I wanted more for myself and others.

When I entered Lowndes County Training School the first day of my senior year, the halls appeared narrower and the rooms seemed smaller. The deficits in my education were more glaring than ever. But glimmers of hope were all around in the form of good, earnest teachers.

English teacher Coley Whiting looked like a nerd with his horn-rimmed glasses and pockets full of pens, but he was a quiet revolutionary. He brought the classics to life and introduced us to non-traditional literature like *The Autobiography of Malcolm X*. Johnny Stanford taught algebra I and II, geometry, and trigonometry. His class was so enjoyable that we didn't want it to end. We'd gather in the library afterward to discuss formulas and do computations. Theresa Gardner Douglas captured our imaginations in physics and chemistry. Sometimes I wonder how many future scientists she would have inspired if she'd had the proper equipment. I did not even see a microscope until my freshman year in college, but I considered a science major because of her.

After Principal Pierce's removal, my popularity grew, and I was elected vice president of the senior class. Outside of school, my father and I regularly attended school board meetings along with Arlinda's father, Rev. Knight. Our group, Concerned Parents and Students for Quality Education, had formed alliances with three of the five school board members. Two were Black—and I admired their courage, gallantry, and strength. The days of "Bloody Lowndes," when Black people could be lynched for standing up to white rule, were not far behind us. Many older people had never learned to read and still signed their names with an "X."

Our other ally was Mary Dora Hammonds, the wife of Probate Judge Harold Hammonds, who was the largest landowner in Lowndes County. Unlike many of his white counterparts, Judge Hammonds had seen the writing on the wall and begun to work with newly enfranchised Black voters. Since they made up the majority of voters in the county, his position was assured until he decided to give it up.

Mrs. Hammonds was not intimidated by the local white power structure. She was the epitome of an older southern belle. She often called me, and we had long conversations on the telephone. She would even invite me into her home, an old, unkempt southern mansion. When she spoke to me she stood so close that I could feel her breathe. She seemed to feel a level of comfort in my presence that was uncommon among whites and Blacks in Lowndes County.

Our group would meet at the AFSC offices in Montgomery or at the home of Sarah Logan, the teacher who'd sheltered Arlinda and me the day Arlinda was attacked at our high school. With her long hair pulled tightly into a bun, she appeared grandmotherly, but she was a warrior who stood fiercely for Black children.

We considered who should be the next principal and settled on Mr. Sellers, the longtime assistant principal and the administrator that students most respected. Tall, handsome, and robust, he was a commanding figure. He took an interest in my college plans and my writing and sought my opinion on decisions affecting students. He brought order to the chaos that Pierce had allowed. When he walked the halls, students scattered.

Our group's next priority was replacing Hulda Coleman as superintendent of schools. Coleman's father had been superintendent of schools before her, and she had basically inherited the position from him. It was common knowledge that her brother had shot and killed white seminarian and voting rights activist Jonathan Daniels during the height of the civil rights movement in Lowndes County, only to be acquitted.

Coleman was petite, with a calm presence. She had been Pierce's ally, but she was cordial and polite to me, in the southern way. She had even hired my mother to work as a teacher's aide. But she had allowed troubling disparities between Black and white schools during segregation and permitted the chaos at our high school. She only had a bachelor's degree, while most of the Black teachers had earned master's degrees. Most people on her administrative staff were white, and resources were not equitably distributed.

At the first school board meeting that year, I asked for an investigation of Coleman's violations of the Alabama School Code. To our surprise, she said she was resigning. She looked across the room at my father and me and walked out of the meeting. Her calm veneer had cracked.

We were surprised, but were also prepared with a recommendation for her successor. Euralee Haynes was well respected, came from a family that had been active in the civil rights movement, and had the credentials necessary to do the job. A board majority approved, and Mrs. Haynes became the first Black superintendent of schools for Lowndes County.

Although Mrs. Coleman's resignation was the highlight of the meeting, I stuck with my plan to ask for the name of the high school to be changed. One of the white board members said I should be proud to attend a school that bore the last name of William Yancey Lowndes, the confederate slave owner who had led the walkout of southern states from the Union and for whom Lowndes County was named. One of the lessons I had learned from my summer at the Robert Kennedy Memorial Foundation was to be prepared with counterattacks, so I responded that the name was a vestige of segregation. The board voted to appoint a committee to gauge community support for the name change and to find a name that was acceptable to all. I was asked to serve on that committee.

High school had long been a luxury for sharecroppers' children, and many students in my class were the first in their families to graduate. It was a significant milestone. It was customary for the senior class to leave the school a gift, and the one we chose was close to my heart: we raised money to pay for our school's new name to be placed on the building. Even more important to me was that my diploma would not say Lowndes County Training School. It would say Central High School instead.

A week later, I began summer school at Alabama State University.

Chapter 3

Alabama State University (ASU) was not my first choice for college. I wanted to go to Howard University, a private school in Washington, DC. It was often called the "Black Harvard," and it boasted Stokely Carmichael and other SNCC members as alumni. But my father urged me to attend ASU because it was in Montgomery, closer to home, and it was an affordable state school. As a compromise, I chose to attend ASU for the summer, but accepted a full scholarship in the fall to Talladega College, a small historically Black school about fifty miles east of Birmingham. Recruiters for the school had set their sights on me when I was in the tenth grade. Because of my grades, I could have gone there at the end of eleventh grade instead of returning to school in Lowndes County, but my parents had vetoed that possibility. Knowing that I might have some deficits, I registered for summer school at ASU to get an early start.

ASU was founded by nine ex-slaves at the end of the Civil War in Marion, Alabama, as Lincoln Normal School. It was renamed the State Normal School and University for the Education of Colored Teachers and Students in 1873 when it came under control of the state. It evolved into the Alabama State

College for Negroes in 1948, Alabama State College in 1954, and finally Alabama State University in 1969.

I arrived in June 1976 full of wonder and hope for this new season of my life. My first night on campus, I sat on the block in front of my dorm, Bibb Graves Hall, the oldest dorm on campus. It was named for Alabama governor David Bibb Graves, who was considered one of the state's most liberal governors of the twentieth century. Two upperclassmen approached me, one from Philadelphia and the other from Detroit. They were members of the university's famed Marching Hornets band. Philly, as William Boynton was fondly known, was a giant compared to my five feet two inches, and he smiled easily. When he found out I was only seventeen, he told me that my new name was Baby Sister and he would introduce me to everyone that way. Philly's family had cemented their role in civil rights history. His grandmother, Amelia Boynton Robinson, was a leader of the fight for voting rights in Selma, and was beaten unconscious during Bloody Sunday on the Edmund Pettus Bridge in 1965. His Uncle Bruce was the plaintiff in the landmark case *Boynton v. Virginia*, which was argued by Thurgood Marshall—later the first Black Supreme Court justice.

Bruce Boynton was a Howard University law student traveling home to Selma on a Trailways bus in 1958. When the bus stopped in Richmond, he tried to buy a cheeseburger in the whites-only section of the bus station restaurant. He was arrested and convicted of trespassing in a verdict that was overturned by the United States Supreme Court in 1960. The majority opinion, written by Justice Hugo Black, held that racial segregation in public transportation was illegal. That led directly to the Freedom Rides, launched the next year when mixed-race groups rode buses to the South to test enforcement of the ruling. They incurred brutal attacks in Montgomery and elsewhere until the federal government stepped in.

I'd expected college to be a different world from high school, but clearly I would never be far from the civil rights movement.

I carried a full load that summer, which was a total of five classes. Some were very small, giving me close contact with my professors. One whom I found intriguing was Miss Bernice Hollinger, a middle-aged English professor who spoke with precise diction. Wearing horn-rimmed glasses and classic suits, she spent the first day of class getting to know her three students. I was the youngest. The other female student worked as a maid while she pursued a teaching degree and raised her children. The gentleman in our class was bright but had learning challenges. I was moved by how much time Miss Hollinger spent with him. She met his enthusiasm for learning with determination to help him reach his goal. Her example would later influence me when I became a teacher.

For the class we read *Jonathan Livingston Seagull* by Richard Bach. I enjoyed the book's message of finding one's own way. Jonathan had to choose between conforming to the seagull's expected way of life or taking flight on a different path. That choice resonated with me.

After summer session ended, I went on to Talladega College, Alabama's oldest private Black college. It began in 1867 as Swayne School in a building slaves had built originally for white students. The charter for Talladega College was issued in 1869, and history lived on in its oldest buildings. Thirty-two of the buildings are listed on the National Historic Registry, and I could practically hear the echoes of the past as I walked their halls. Enrollment was so small that we joked that we could all see and talk to each other at least three times a day. It was friendly and welcoming.

The student body was all Black, yet diverse. At Talladega I first became aware of the term "Geechee," used to describe African Americans from the Lowcountry of coastal South

Carolina and Georgia. Many students came from Charleston, and their accents were distinctive. Other students were from the West Coast or Midwest, some of them following in their parents' and grandparents' footsteps. We were often reminded that Talladega was one of the best colleges to attend to get into graduate school. I was still considering going to law school, so that was music to my ears.

Talladega was a small town, and most of our activity outside class was on campus. I joined a group supporting the Wilmington Ten, a group of young Black people wrongly convicted of arson and conspiracy during a night of unrest in Wilmington, NC. They were sentenced to a total of 282 years in prison. My professor and advisor, Dr. Bernie Bray, had taught one of the Ten, and he made sure we knew about them.

As a white political science professor teaching at a historically Black university, Dr. Bray had a unique perspective, and he strongly encouraged my activism. His sense of justice was infectious. He had arrived at Talladega in 1971, seven years before I graduated from high school, to develop a political science program. By the time I met him he was legendary.

Through the story of the Wilmington Ten, I was introduced to the term "political prisoners." Their cause attracted international attention as an example of racial injustice in America. That fall, a march was planned in Raleigh, the capital of North Carolina, in support of the group, and several buses were traveling there from Talladega College. I decided to go.

We left for North Carolina early in the morning. I slept most of the way, until we stopped at a truck stop for a bathroom and food break. When one of the students was served coffee in a dirty cup, we were rounded up to return to the bus and leave. It was a sign of what to expect once we arrived in Raleigh.

The crowds in Raleigh were very large. I had never seen law enforcement so massively armed, and it was intimidating. We had been told not to engage in violence, and I do not recall even any civil disobedience. We heard from an array of speakers, and near the end of the day, a popular entertainer, Billy Paul, came to the mike to speak and perform. He was best known for "Me and Mrs. Jones," a number one hit in 1972 and a Grammy Award winner. I liked it because I love smooth jazz, but I wouldn't get to hear the whole song. The sound was cut off mid-song, and I wondered if that was intended to be a provocation. Fortunately, it was near the end of the day. Everyone retained their composure and returned grumbling to the buses.

The Wilmington Ten's convictions eventually were overturned. One of them, Benjamin Chavis, wrote two books during his ten years' imprisonment, and went on to earn a master's degree in divinity from Duke University and a doctorate in ministry from Howard before becoming executive director of the NAACP.

I wasn't at Talladega College for long. The time I spent at ASU had made me a fan of the band and the football team, and Talladega had neither. It seemed like every weekend ASU played a home game, I was in Montgomery, and the trips back and forth by Trailways bus over narrow roads and bridges were hard. When my father asked if I wanted to return to ASU, I jumped at the chance.

Soon I'd change colleges again. I was only at ASU for one semester when I had a chance to attend Howard University, my dream school. David Hackett arranged for me to receive a stipend from the Robert F. Kennedy Memorial that would cover the cost of tuition, room, and board. My father was not happy, but I packed my bags the fall of 1977 to move to Washington, DC.

Howard was everything that I dreamed it would be, with students from around the world. It was my first time encountering wealthy Black students. As much as I enjoyed being a student there, I became incredibly self-conscious that I was poor and very rural—a country girl. Many students dressed in designer clothes and drove luxury cars. While sitting in the lounge, I could hear them talking about their summer excursions to Europe. This was foreign to me.

I was trying to figure out where I fit in when I saw a flyer advertising a seminar about the Allan Bakke case. Still very much an activist, I decided to attend. The Bakke case challenged affirmative action in higher education. Allan Bakke, a white student, applied to medical school at the University of California at Davis and was rejected. He sued, alleging discrimination because Black students with lower test scores and grades than his were admitted. There was concern this case would undo affirmative action on college campuses nationwide, and I wanted to learn as much as I could about it.

The speaker that night was Dr. Herbert O. Reid, a professor at Howard's law school. He talked about the legal implications of the case and also referenced a case at Alabama State University. I asked questions during the seminar and mentioned my past activism. Afterward, I introduced myself. Dr. Reid looked at me attentively as I told him I was from Lowndes County and had attended ASU. He said, "Young lady, there is a case involving Alabama State University that could have similar implications for affirmative action."

The case was *Craig v. Alabama State University*, a class action suit alleging discrimination against white employees in promotion and tenure decisions. Dr. Reid said that many people did not realize how important this case was and it would be great if I could help people understand the threat to Black institutions of higher learning. I told him that I would be happy to return to ASU to help with this cause if I could, but school had already started and I would have to wait until the spring.

He said that Dr. Levi Watkins, the president, was a friend of his, and he asked for my contact information.

The next day, I was sitting in my dorm room waiting to go to class when my phone rang. Dr. Watkins was on the other end. He had served as ASU president during some turbulent times in the fight for civil rights. If I had been there then, I would surely have been one of the students he suspended for participating in civil disobedience. Yet now he was calling after hearing about me from Reid. He told me that the future of ASU was being threatened and he wanted me to help in the fight to save the school if I returned to ASU. He said to see him if I decided to come back. In a few days I was on a bus returning to Montgomery.

I went to see Dr. Watkins, and he cleared the way for me to re-enroll at ASU. We began to meet about once a month in his conference room. Dr. Watkins was a handsome middle-aged Black gentleman who was so light-skinned that at first glance he appeared to be white. He would peer over his wire-rimmed glasses, which were en vogue at the time, and talk in his deliberate cadence about his tenure at the university. We often talked about the Bakke case, and he also discussed the incredible strides his children were making. His son, Dr. Levi Watkins Jr., was a gifted cardiovascular surgeon, and the senior Dr. Watkins beamed with pride, recalling how Levi Jr. was offered the chance to practice under heart transplant pioneer Dr. Christiaan Barnard in South Africa. A child of the civil rights movement, the younger Watkins turned down the option to become an honorary white person in apartheid South Africa and instead practiced at Johns Hopkins University.

Dr. Watkins believed in the importance of historically Black colleges and universities, or HBCUs, in helping Black students who came from school systems plagued with inequalities. He worried that the Craig case threatened ASU's right to exist as an HBCU. He knew my history as an activist in Lowndes

County and during my brief time at ASU, where I once led a demonstration against the student union. He knew students would follow me, and he wanted me to understand his position.

A federal court ruled against ASU in the *Craig* case in 1978. The university survived it, but another threat was on the horizon. Talk was beginning to circulate in political circles about merging the three state-supported universities in Montgomery—ASU, Auburn University in Montgomery (AUM), and Troy State University—into a proposed University of Montgomery.

Many of us worried about ASU being dissolved and disappearing. Black teachers and administrators had lost their jobs when Black public schools merged into white ones during desegregation, and we were concerned that this paradigm would play out at the university level if we remained silent. We would lose teachers like Miss Bernice Hollinger, the English teacher who had inspired me that first summer at ASU, and so much more. Historically Black colleges and universities provide a safe place for students to learn with others from similar backgrounds. We learned about the achievements of Black people in a way that was not then taught at predominantly white schools. We treasured our rich culture—including our renowned marching band.

I decided to express my feelings by putting pen to paper. A little more than a year after leaving high school, I wrote a letter to the *Alabama Journal*, one of two daily Montgomery newspapers. The letter was published on November 9, 1977, and entitled "Bad Ole Hornet:"

To the Journal:
It is to my dismay that every time I pick up an issue of the Journal I see very few positive articles, if any, about Alabama State University. As a student at ASU I would

like to shed some light on the real issue concerning my school. In the days of segregation it was not popular for black children to be educated with whites; therefore most of those ended up in inferior institutions called training schools.

As recent as 1968 black children went to school in facilities that resembled the old classrooms I saw on display at the Smithsonian Institute. Children from these institutions were not acceptable to white institutions of higher learning, so they had to attend black institutions like ASU. The selection of a president of those institutions was as important to whites as to blacks. First of all, if a radical person was selected, sooner or later, he would be replaced by what many of us term as a "Tom" to occupy the seat.

I congratulate Dr. Levi Watkins for being conservative enough to please his white superiors and being smart enough to increase the size of the campus. Tomming is no longer in style and black schools are no longer fashionable. When will everyone realize that the real issue concerning ASU is racism? Never have I seen a negative article about AUM. A clear illustration of racism is the building of AUM while ASU was there all the time. Where were all of the so-called liberals presently screaming merger, when AUM was being planned?

I think that it is about time for education to become more important than politics. I am not upholding anyone at ASU in any wrongdoing. I will be one of the first to complain when the quality of my education is endangered. Hopefully, this Bakke mania will phase out soon . . .

All that had happened—meeting Dr. Reed, talking with Dr. Watkins, and learning that ASU could be dissolved—placed me on a course of organizing that was new to me. I had a strong desire for higher education. I was young and loved to dance and write and enjoy all that college had to offer, but my passion for justice would always usurp whatever else was going on in my life.

Still very much the free-spirited activist, I was in and out of school based on what movement needed my attention and labor. I began learning how to mobilize large groups, a skill I'd call on later when the need to preserve ASU became urgent. But that would take a few years. Meanwhile, I was still finding myself and figuring out what I wanted to do with my life. In 1978, feeling burned out from the fight against injustice and needing a break from school, I joined the Air National Guard, and after basic training and technical school, I joined the regular Air Force in 1979. I became a victim of sexual harassment and left the service in 1980. You could say I was part of the "me too" movement before there was a movement.

I returned to ASU as a student in 1980 and found the issue of merging universities still alive, led by then Governor Fob James. I began to know some emerging power brokers in local and state government. John Knight, the public relations director at ASU whose name would become a symbol of education reform in Alabama, was like an older brother to me. I'd talk to him about political action, and he'd try to temper my youthful exuberance, often unsuccessfully. Joe Reed was a Montgomery city councilman who'd later become a dominant figure in the Alabama Democratic Party. I'd met him when I was in high school and, as the president of the teachers association, he'd represented the suspended principal, Dr. Pierce. On campus, I started partnering with Randy Anderson, a student and Vietnam veteran, in organizing students for political causes.

Randy's and my work got the attention of Reed and Knight,

and they summoned us to a meeting. Reed had been the strategist behind many court cases that had expanded voting rights to Black Alabamans. Now, facing the threat to ASU, he had developed a strategy that went beyond marching and drew on some hard facts.

In 1980, a report from the United States Department of Education Civil Rights Compliance Unit had found that Alabama still maintained vestiges of segregation in higher education. This was not unexpected. At one time, Black college graduates seeking graduate degrees had to leave the state to be educated, at the state's expense. Autherine Lucy, the first Black student to be admitted to the University of Alabama in 1956, was expelled when riots broke out on campus protesting her presence. In June of 1963, George Wallace stood in the schoolhouse door to protest Vivian Malone's admission to the University of Alabama. He was ordered to move by the Alabama National Guard, which was federalized by President John Kennedy that same month. Now, in 1981, we were still fighting, but at least the federal court offered a fairer playing field, and the federal report gave us ammunition.

At the meeting, Randy and I learned we had been selected to be plaintiffs in a lawsuit to save ASU. We would represent students; Knight and professors John Gibson and Alma Freeman would represent alumni. Reed led the discussion, and attorney Donald Watkins was also present. Donald, the son of ASU's president, Dr. Levi Watkins, had been one of the first Black students to desegregate the law school at the University of Alabama.

The lawsuit asked that the two other universities in Montgomery—Troy State and Auburn in Montgomery—be merged into ASU. Instead of the new entity that the governor proposed, there would be one larger ASU. The lawsuit aimed to save ASU and also to end the remnants of segregation that lived on in the separate versions of the same programs provided by the three schools. We were told that the name of the plaintiff listed first on the case would brand the case, and John Knight asked for that position. We all agreed, and the suit was filed in federal court on January 15, 1981. At a press conference that day, Reed pointed out that of the three schools, ASU was by far the oldest, with the most established traditions. ASU was more than one hundred years old, while the other two were newcomers, having only arrived in the mid-1960s.

Meanwhile, Randy and I and other friends organized a march to save ASU. We were joined by the Southern Christian Leadership Conference as well as students from all of the HBCUs in Alabama. On February 19, 1981, a crowd estimated at fifteen hundred to three thousand people marched from the ASU campus to the state capital. The local newspaper called our march one of the largest in Montgomery since the days of the civil rights movement. This was exciting for us because it was mostly organized by students.

The Knight case, as it would become known, would last almost thirty years and expose long-standing racist practices governing education in Alabama. It would ultimately include more plaintiffs, more issues, and more attorneys. It argued that Alabama's very method of funding K–12 education and HBCUs was discriminatory, and federal courts agreed. The three universities were never merged, but courts ordered numerous changes in state policy.

ASU survives today, more than one hundred fifty years after its founding. I feel proud knowing that I had a hand in laying the groundwork for the eventual resolution of the case.

My passion for justice was as strong as ever after the march, and I became an active member of SCLC. At that time, the distinguished civil rights leader Dr. Joseph Lowery was president. I was moved by Dr. Lowery's eloquent speeches and commanding presence. Often, he was surrounded by advisors like R.B. Cottonreader and Reverend Albert Love, and I would watch them, imagining what it must have been like to sit with Jesus and his disciples.

I came to Dr. Lowery's attention when I helped organize the march to save ASU and the establishment of an SCLC chapter on campus. Whenever Dr. Lowery or others from his team called me to mobilize for a demonstration, I organized a student cohort to go there.

We marched in Mobile after the lynching of Michael Donald, who was chosen randomly for execution by Klan members who wanted to intimidate the Black community. Members of the United Klans of America, one of the largest Ku Klux Klan organizations in the country, were angry because the trial of a Black man accused of killing a white police officer had ended in a mistrial. In retaliation, they abducted nineteen-year-old Donald as he walked to the store. They beat him, cut his throat, and then hung him from a tree.

What happened next shows why activism is so vital to the cause of justice. Local police didn't look seriously into Donald's lynching, but demonstrations helped keep the case alive. Finally, two Klansmen were arrested and convicted of the murder. Then, the Southern Poverty Law Center sued the United Klans on behalf of Donald's mother and won a $7 million judgment. That bankrupted the United Klans, whose legacy of terror included brutal attacks on Freedom Riders in 1961, the bombing of Birmingham's 16th Street Baptist Church in 1963 in which four girls were killed, and the murder of civil rights volunteer Viola Liuzzo in Lowndes County in 1965.

Another march made a deep impact on me and changed the

trajectory of my life. It was organized in 1982 to protest the arrests and convictions of Maggie Bozeman and Julia Wilder in Pickens County, which sits along Alabama's border with Mississippi. Wilder, aged sixty-nine, president of the Pickens County Voters League, and Bozeman, fifty-one, president of the county's NAACP chapter, were accused of mishandling absentee ballots they had gathered from elderly and illiterate Black voters in a local election. Tried and convicted by an all-white jury despite shaky evidence, the two Black women received harsh sentences: the maximum five years for Wilder and four years for Bozeman.

Two years later, the verdicts would be overturned, but the immediate reaction was outrage. A crowd of nearly three hundred mostly Black spectators reacted with shock to the sentencing, some rising and singing the old civil rights movement standard "We Shall Not Be Moved," despite the judge's call for order. Supporters of the women organized a 180-mile march that would start in Pickens County and end in Montgomery, passing through Selma on the way.

Rose Sanders, a local activist and civil rights attorney, had invited me to Selma to see a play she had written and produced, so I joined up with the marchers there. I had known Rose since high school because her husband, Hank Sanders, had represented our group, the Concerned Parents and Students for Quality Education. After the play, Rose and I attended a mass meeting at Brown Chapel AME Church, which was the starting point of the historic Selma-to-Montgomery march with Dr. King. Dr. Lowery was speaking, acknowledging all the different groups that were present. Someone in the balcony shouted out, "Georgia State University!" I looked to see who the voice belonged to and saw an attractive brown-skinned young woman standing up. She was "Able" Mable

Thomas, and she would become a close, lifelong friend. Today, she is a Georgia state legislator.

The next day, I joined the march. It was my first time marching those fifty-four miles to Montgomery. I was unprepared but determined to walk every step of the way. It was a powerful experience. When I initially set out, I was wearing boots. I soon learned that was the quickest way to develop blisters and sore feet. Somebody lent me a pair of tennis shoes until I could go home and get appropriate footwear. Some days it rained, and some days it was hot, but our sense of purpose eclipsed any physical discomfort.

At night, many of the marchers slept in churches. Since my parents lived nearby and I shared a house with a roommate in Montgomery, I only stayed in a church once, and it was a night to remember. People from the community brought more than enough food for the marchers to eat, and veterans of the movement shared eye-opening and inspiring stories. I felt that this was a historic moment much bigger than myself.

The bonding that took place along the way was indescribable. I met longtime movement hero Reverend James Orange, who'd been an assistant to Dr. King. Someone told me Dr. King had given him the nickname "Shackdaddy." He was a gentle giant, about six feet tall and three hundred pounds, with a wonderful singing voice. He'd lead songs along the way, each one telling a story about the movement, and whenever we stopped, he'd give us a history lesson about wherever we happened to be. We called him Big Leader, but he called everybody else leaders. I only found out later what a pivotal role he played in civil rights history.

In early 1965, James had been convicted and jailed in Perry County, Alabama, for contributing to the delinquency of minors after recruiting young people to help with voter registration. There was talk that James was going to be lynched, and his supporters turned out for a night march to try to stop his execution. They'd barely left the church where they'd assembled for the march when state troopers savagely attacked them. During the melee, a young Vietnam veteran and church deacon named Jimmy Lee Jackson hurried his mother and grandfather into a restaurant to take shelter from the violence. State police followed them, and one of them shot and killed Jackson in cold blood. News of this horrific act helped trigger a series of crucial events: Bloody Sunday, the Selma to Montgomery march, and, ultimately, the passage of the landmark Voting Rights Act.

James became a close associate of Dr. King over the next three years and was standing at the bottom of the stairs at the Lorraine Motel in Memphis when Dr. King was assassinated in 1968. He kept up his social justice work for the rest of his life. Our paths crossed many times over the years, and James became a lifelong friend and mentor to me.

I also met Tony Liuzzo. Tony's mother, Viola Liuzzo, a white woman from Detroit, went to Selma before the first march to help with voter registration. After the march ended in Montgomery, she was giving a young Black man a ride back to Selma when a car full of Klansmen spotted them in Lowndes County. They fired into the car, killing Viola. We stopped with Tony to lay a wreath at the place on Highway 80 where she'd died, now memorialized by a historical marker.

As we walked through Lowndes County, people who lived there would join us. James Orange and Leon Hall, who'd been a youth coordinator for Dr. King during the original march, were surprised that I knew so many of them, and they asked me to speak at one of the churches. I don't remember much about my speech, but I had grown up speaking in churches in Lowndes County, and it was great to be home where the audience responded with applause and shouts of "Amen!" They might have been moved by the fact I was a local girl speaking among these giants. Whatever the reason, the reaction prompted James to pull me aside and suggest that I consider running for public office in Lowndes County. This had never crossed my mind, but the thought stayed with me.

When we set out on the road to Montgomery, our goal was to follow the original route of the Selma to Montgomery march, including the portion in downtown Montgomery along Dexter Avenue, past the church where Dr. King had preached. There was a problem, though. Montgomery mayor Emory Folmar said we would not be able to march the original route and would have to take a more circuitous one. We began to anticipate a confrontation.

I had a chance to see leadership in action when Dr. Lowery pulled me out of the march and asked me to join him in a meeting in Montgomery with the editorial board of the *Alabama Journal*. He explained to me the importance of telling the local press why we were marching. Later, I joined him in a meeting with union organizers, who assured us they would provide bail money for anyone arrested if we had a conflict over the route. Unions had historically backed the civil rights movement, including in Lowndes County, where unions from Michigan lent their support.

The drama reached a crescendo on the final day of the march. Approximately two thousand people walked that day. People continued to join us, including students from a high school we passed. Elementary students waved from their school. Shoppers left stores to walk with us, and shop owners proudly put "Closed" signs on their doors and fell in too. This march was not just about freeing Mrs. Wilder and Mrs. Bozeman. It was also about voting rights.

I served as a marshal that day, flanking the front line that was packed with famous civil rights leaders. The scene is still so vivid in my mind that I can even remember how I was dressed: in blue jeans with a light blue shirt and borrowed sneakers, my hair in individual long braids. Behind me were John Knight and Mrs. Johnnie Carr. She was the long-serving president of the Montgomery Improvement Association, the organization that had led the Montgomery bus boycott after Rosa Parks was arrested for refusing to give her seat to a white man.

When we topped the hill overlooking downtown Montgomery and the state capitol building, we could see police officers in riot gear waiting for us. I braced myself, not knowing what to expect. We'd had a mighty prayer service the night before, and I knew I could be beaten, jailed, or both. But on this journey I had learned the power of prayer and nonviolent protest. We kept walking.

As we approached the line of police, Dr. Lowery stopped the marchers to pray. Then we moved forward. John Knight reached for me and told me to get behind him. I knew that if the police attacked us, I could be killed. Just before we reached the point of decision, where we could go the approved route or follow the historic path, Dr. Lowery steered us to the approved path. The confrontation was avoided. I heard sighs of relief, and I also heard swearing from people who were ready to resist an unjust order even if it meant a beating and jail.

The night before, we'd been instructed to write down the names of three people we could call if we were arrested. I'd written my parents' names and also Rose Sanders, since she was an attorney. I knew I could reach them if I needed them. It turned out I wouldn't have had to call. When we arrived at the capitol, I was surprised to see them all there. My father wasn't the type to march, but he explained that he wanted to be nearby if I needed him. I felt very blessed to have such love and support at a moment like this, when adrenaline was pumping and anything could have happened.

Justice moves and inspires people to stand up in different ways. You don't have to march to have a huge impact on those who do. This was another lesson in my education as an activist.

Chapter 4

After the march to Montgomery, I decided to take James Orange's advice and run for public office in Lowndes County. The position I chose was circuit court clerk. I enjoyed meeting people on the campaign trail, but otherwise I did not like the process of running for office. For one thing, it involved going to every possible event to solicit support. I also learned I was better at promoting others than myself. After I lost to the incumbent, I decided that I needed a change of pace.

James and I had discussed the possibility of an internship at the Martin Luther King Jr. Center for Nonviolent Social Change in Atlanta, and that's where I ended up going. My job was to research the role of students in the civil rights movement, using the King Center's archives, which were full of information. I also had a chance to reconnect with Mable Thomas, whom I'd gotten to know on the march. Mable attended Georgia State in Atlanta, and was active in student government and the Black Student Union. She'd organized a group of students to help canvas Lowndes County during my campaign, and we'd become close friends.

In Atlanta, I visited Mable often. Students would gather

in the living room of her one-bedroom apartment, which was decorated with posters of art by Black artists and stocked with books by Black authors. When there weren't enough chairs we'd sit on the floor and talk into the night about social and political issues until the downstairs neighbor thumped on the ceiling with her broom handle. Like me, Mable was inspired by James Orange. He advised her to run for office, and in 1984 she won a seat in the state legislature, where she still serves. She was one of many courageous young people that I met during my time there.

Atlanta was so inspiring that I decided to stay on after my internship ended. I went to work in the director's office of the Georgia Department of Public Health. In some ways, Atlanta was like Montgomery, but it was more of a Black mecca. It was home to a number of historically Black colleges and universities—Morehouse, Spelman, Clark, and Morris Brown, in addition to Georgia State—and many progressive student groups.

There was a sense of excitement that we were entering a new era. Andrew Young, a civil rights leader who'd become a congressman from Georgia and then United States ambassador to the United Nations, had recently been elected mayor. Everyone I met boasted about being a member of the "Blue Crew," young people who campaigned for Young. Blue was also the color of the signs used in the campaign.

In Atlanta, I had a certain degree of anonymity that I did not have in Montgomery. No one knew me. I was just like everybody else. That allowed me freedom to be a young person in a way that was new to me. I could participate in activities without being expected to lead them. There were many leaders there, and I could simply be a servant.

There were clubs where I could go dancing. Or I could just

explore the city. I spent hundreds of dollars at a Black bookstore called Hakim's that carried stacks of books on Black history and culture. Nearby on Martin Luther King Drive was Paschal's Motel, where civil rights leaders had gathered to strategize in the early days of the movement. It was not unusual to run into people around town like Hosea Williams, E. Randall Osborne, or John Lewis, all pioneers in the struggle for voting and social rights in Atlanta and around the nation.

It was a dream come true to be in the presence of Rev. King's widow, Coretta Scott King, who was just as elegant in person as she was in pictures. Daddy King, Rev. King's father, was still alive then and living in Atlanta. A few steps away from the King Center was Ebenezer Baptist Church, where Rev. King had preached. Walking through the historic Auburn Avenue neighborhood, once home to the nation's largest concentration of Black-owned businesses, I passed a well-maintained row of houses where elderly Black women stopped me to ask where I was from. We talked about life in rural Lowndes County, and they told me stories of Rev. King growing up in their neighborhood. This was fascinating to me.

Many of my friends from Alabama and other places would come to visit me during my tenure there. On a Saturday in December of 1984, I was awaiting two friends, one driving from Alabama and the other on a bus from Columbus, Georgia, and I passed the time by doing laundry. Sitting in the busy laundromat while my clothes dried, I looked up from my newspaper to see a young man come in and head for a pay phone. Our eyes met, and I smiled at him because he was wearing a uniform. I had huge respect for the military since my father had served and two of my siblings had signed up. It was a way for Black people to enter the middle class, putting them on a path toward home ownership, civil service jobs, and college.

I returned to my newspaper and didn't notice the young man had approached me until he said, "Excuse me, I know it is too soon for me to ask you to marry me." I smiled at the lame pick-up line and responded, "Yes, it is, but you can have my phone number." That was the beginning of a long-distance courtship that led to our getting married in July 1985.

His name was Thurgood Bunche Flowers. We were married in a gazebo overlooking the river at Holy Ground, a site sacred to the Red Stick Creek Indians in Lowndes County. His mother had named him for Nobel laureate Ralph Bunche and Supreme Court Justice Thurgood Marshall. He did not like his name much, but I would always tell him that his mother had named him for great men of her time, hoping they would inspire him. Thurgood had attended school at the University of North Carolina Charlotte and, like me, had not finished college. He decided instead to join the army and was a cannon fire direction specialist in field artillery, stationed at Fort Sill, Oklahoma.

After our wedding, we moved there. Fort Sill is about eighty-five miles north of Oklahoma City. It once was home to the 10th Calvary, a distinguished regiment of former slaves called Buffalo soldiers. It was also famous for housing Geronimo and other Apache prisoners of war. There were still signs of indigenous and frontier life.

The rugged beauty of the area was intoxicating, with mountains in the background and a brilliant display of stars in the night sky. Prairie dogs and armadillos roamed the landscape. The weather, colder than that in the Southeast, took some getting used to. So did my new role.

Being a military wife was new for me, and I was soon bored.

I had not made friends yet, and I didn't have a job. I wasn't accustomed to having so much time on my hands. It seemed like the perfect time to go back to school. There would be no distractions, I thought. Cameron University was less than ten minutes from our apartment, and I was twenty-five hours away from my degree in history and political science. A counselor at the university assured me that if all went well, I would graduate the next spring.

The first day of class, I went to the campus full of purpose, feeling overjoyed that I was on the last stretch of my college education. Once my classes ended, I drove home to wait to hear from my husband, who was in the field training with his platoon. But when my phone rang, a strange voice was on the other end. It was a doctor asking me to come to the post hospital. He said my husband had been in an accident, but he was okay. What he said next felt like a scene from a soap opera: "He may not remember you, because he has amnesia."

This was exactly two months after Thurgood and I had said our vows. I wondered whether someone was playing tricks on me. I had only heard about amnesia on television. Could this be real? I wondered. I drove to the hospital in my Ford Escort and met with the doctor. He said that a tent pole had snapped loose and popped my husband between the eyes. Initially, Thurgood told his superiors he was okay. Then he lost consciousness and was taken to the hospital. Now he was conscious but out of it, although he realized he had suffered a head injury, the doctor said. The doctor thought a few days at home would help him heal so he could return to duty.

When I entered the room where Thurgood was lying in a hospital bed, the doctor told him I was his wife. His eyes widened in bewilderment and I could tell that he did not recognize me. He told me I was pretty as if I were a stranger. It was surreal. That evening he was released from the hospital to go home with me. While we were in the parking lot, I stepped back waiting for him to approach our car. He stopped and looked at me. He did not know which car was ours. I drove home, still in a state of shock. I watched him walk around our apartment looking as if he were seeing it for the first time. I felt like I was with a stranger.

This was a challenge I did not know if I was prepared to address. Newly married to a husband with a head injury, living in a new part of the United States, and taking a full load of classes during my final year in college, I had to regroup. First, I was determined I would finish school. Second, I had to learn as much as I could about amnesia and head injuries. And finally, I had to learn how to help my husband regain his memory and handle whatever deficits might remain.

We adjusted, and fortunately he trusted me to make decisions. When he had to return to duty, it was another reality. He did not remember how to get to work, so the first day, I drove him. I didn't want to leave him there, and I even spoke to one of his commanders about it. No one seemed to take my concerns seriously. I went home, anxious, and stayed near the phone.

It was approaching noon when I received the call to come and get him. I was told that he'd had a breakdown at work because he did not remember anyone or anything. He was taken to the hospital again and then released to rest a few more days at home. The doctors kept saying there was no evidence on the brain scans that he had suffered any injury, and suggested that he was malingering. It was the first time I'd hear that term applied to his condition. I requested that he be seen by a head injury specialist.

The National Head Injury Foundation gave me lots of

information to help me understand Thurgood's condition. My background as an activist and advocate helped guide us through this period. His commanders accepted that he was pretending instead of believing the evidence in front of their faces. Many of them had been in the field with him when the accident occurred. Yet when their man was down, they did not support him. I enlisted his family and friends in that effort. It was several weeks, but he began to slowly regain his memory. The headaches never went away. I had to adjust to him appearing dazed, experiencing drowsiness and confusion. At home, we were dating again, with him getting to know me. I also had to get to know him and help him navigate this new terrain.

I had seen this play out before during my own time in the military. I had served in the California Air National Guard and then enlisted in the regular air force in Montgomery. Then I was stationed at McConnell Air Force Base in Wichita, Kansas, and that's where I was sexually harassed by my section chief. When I complained, I was not believed. It was easier to believe the victim was lying than to investigate without bias, especially if the victim was a person of color or female. That experience left me with emotional scars that I had to push aside whenever I was asked to help others who were being similarly mistreated.

Now at Fort Sill, with my husband being wronged, I had to act. When I told my mother-in-law what was occurring, she advised me to consider the consequences of speaking out. This was a startling example of the fear people from marginalized communities feel when faced with injustice and inequality. Although her son was in a challenging situation, my new mother-in-law was concerned that my activism on his behalf could lead to retribution. However, my life's experiences up to that point had taught me that looking the other way often led to more injustice. So I called on my father, the seasoned activist and military veteran, to help me navigate this rough patch. He advised me to document everything and to ask questions.

I finally convinced the chain of command to fly us to Brooke Army Hospital in San Antonio, Texas, for Thurgood to be evaluated. We were transported in what seemed to be a cargo plane, devoid of luxuries. Patients lay in beds while other passengers sat in uncomfortable seats. The plane made several stops to pick up patients and family members before landing in San Antonio. There, we were met by a bus with space for beds for the patients. The rest of us sat in seats, wondering what was next.

I stayed in lodging for dependents of military personnel. Most days I spent at the hospital with my books and Thurgood. He was housed in an open bay with other patients.

Thurgood was there nearly three weeks. I was not sure whether he would be discharged from the army or given leave to recover. In addition to amnesia, he began to have terrible headaches. He'd hold his head in his hands, and his eyes would turn red and water. Sometimes he would appear unconscious. It was scary to see, but I had to remain vigilant to advocate for his care.

He saw several doctors at Brooke, including psychologist Brenda Smart. She conducted a battery of tests and concluded that he suffered a closed head injury. He exhibited the classic symptoms: memory loss, headaches, trouble sleeping, dizziness, confusion, and loss of consciousness. But the day he was scheduled to be released from the hospital, there was an unexplained delay in processing his discharge papers. The doctor who oversaw his care came to see him and said he was awaiting the paperwork from Dr. Smart. I offered to go and pick it up.

Dr. Smart gave me the documents in a large envelope and then pulled me aside, out of the earshot of others nearby. She told me that some on the medical team did not want to acknowledge her diagnosis and test results and wanted to believe he was pretending. I thanked her for the information and went by the post library to copy the paperwork before delivering it to the hospital. The attending physician signed the discharge papers and told Thurgood to be prepared to report to work once he returned to Fort Sill.

The day Thurgood was to resume duty, I went to see his commander. He told me that the paperwork said Thurgood was physically sound. He did not resist or question it, although he had been in the field with my husband when the accident occurred. My next stop was the hospital's chief of staff, the lieutenant colonel who had sent Thurgood to Brooke and seemed to possess a sense of fairness. I told him that the diagnosis shared with Thurgood's superiors was not accurate, and I gave him a copy of Dr. Smart's tests and conclusions. He was stunned.

The chief of staff placed Thurgood on leave and ordered a medical board, an independent evaluation by doctors not involved in his care. It was an opportunity to get a review that I hoped would not be tainted by the bias that we were experiencing among some of the military doctors and his chain of command.

In the meantime, the battles did not stop. Unbelievably, Thurgood received orders to go to Germany. Normally, efforts to transfer him would have been on hold while the medical board proceeded. My father called Thurgood's post commander as well as the inspector general at the Pentagon to complain about his son-in-law's treatment. This got the attention of the post commander, whose assistant called to tell me that he did not like that my father had made the call. I told him that my father was a civilian and could call anyone he wanted. I requested, and was granted, a meeting with the entire chain of command.

I was the only woman at the meeting. One Black man, a senior non-commissioned officer, was present. The others were white officers. Pushing aside fear and anxiety, I laid out my case. I had documents backing up each of my claims, and at least one person in the room had been at the scene of the accident. Now I was putting the review board on trial for not assisting a fellow soldier. I asked outright if it was because he was Black.

It was an uncomfortable moment, but I left that meeting with new allies. Each man present had to search internally to understand why he chose to believe the worst of Thurgood, considering the evidence. For a moment I reflected on the systems of slavery and sharecropping in Lowndes County that would not allow a person of color to be sick despite evidence to the contrary. I thought about my mother's sterilization. Thurgood's treatment was an example of victim blaming and shaming, something still prevalent in society today.

I see it when residents of Lowndes and other areas are blamed for their wastewater issues with no consideration that the evidence suggests a greater problem. My husband was simply guilty of a desire to serve his country. In that service, he was injured. Modeling what I had seen exemplified by my family and applying the advocacy skills I had learned in high school, I convinced the medical board that Thurgood was unable to continue his military service. He received a medical discharge.

All these events occurred in less than a year, while I was carrying a heavy college course load. The faculty and administration at Cameron University worked with me, and I completed my studies even while advocating for Thurgood and staying beside him in the hospital.

I had finished my degree program. I also had learned an unforgettable lesson about the audacity needed to challenge structural racism no matter where it appears.

Chapter 5

We had begun our marriage in an unconventional way and decided to continue in that vein. When I was twenty-seven, we moved to Washington, DC, so I could study public interest law. Antioch School of Law had accepted me. However, I arrived in DC to headlines reporting that Antioch was closing. I had to change my plans, and I decided to teach.

My life in DC this time was much different from that when I'd lived with the Hackett family. With them, I'd stayed in tony Chevy Chase and frequented affluent Friendship Heights and Georgetown. I did not see the poorer areas. This time, I learned more about the history of the city and its divisions in income and achievement. The students I would teach came from the most underprivileged parts of the city. Before, I didn't pay attention to the crime rate. Now it was inescapable. I was about to learn another lesson about privilege and the lack of it.

After completing the necessary credentials, I began teaching history and social studies at Shaw Junior High School, once known as "Shameful Shaw," where I'd done my student teaching. The neighborhood was named for Robert Gould Shaw, who'd led the first African American regiment during the Civil

War, the 54th Massachusetts. The school, at Ninth Street and Rhode Island Avenue Northwest, stood near large row homes and a church that was pastored by Walter Fauntroy. Once a major leader of the civil rights movement and the SCLC, Fauntroy had been elected the DC delegate to Congress.

The school building was brick with few windows. The children called it a jail because that's what it looked like from the outside. It was known as a "show school" because of all the officials who visited. On the surface, everything appeared perfect. Appearances were deceiving.

Inside, it was designed as an open space school with no self-contained classrooms. Students were tracked based on their grades and their behavior and sent to corresponding areas. Average performers were assigned to the blue-carpeted Blue House. High achievers went to the Orange House. I taught in the White House, an area in the basement for students with behavioral problems. We were next to the printing shop and special education classes.

During my first week at Shaw, the assistant principal told me that my eighth-grade class had earned more F's than any other class in the school. I found this disclosure disturbing because for most new teachers, such daunting information would create preconceived notions that could influence their teaching. I was determined not to let that deter me, but even the students knew they were not expected to succeed. They were not even allowed to attend programs in the auditorium with other students. They were not disruptive. They had simply been labeled arbitrarily.

My class was large, with more than thirty-five students and not enough books. But turning lemons to lemonade was something I had learned early on in Lowndes County. Besides, I was too hard-headed to let my students fail.

Using reverse psychology, I told my students they were

chosen because they were, in fact, the smartest at the school. I developed a reward system for all who didn't make D's or F's. I created activities and spent my modest pay on workbooks, maps, puzzles, and educational games. I condensed chapters in the few books I had, rewriting them so I could afford to make copies for everyone. The staff at the Kinkos copy center on Capitol Hill began to know me on a first-name basis because I was there so often.

If my students could not go into the auditorium, I would invite guests to come to them. Because we were in the nation's capital, people I knew from Georgia and Alabama were always visiting for conferences or meetings. My guests included Mable Thomas, who by then was a Georgia state representative, and Sheyann Webb-Christburg, who was only nine years old when she'd marched on Bloody Sunday alongside her teacher. Later she co-wrote the book *Selma, Lord, Selma*. I purchased copies for my students, and Sheyann autographed each one.

Dr. Percy Ellis, the principal, noticed that I was bringing guests to my class and students were responding. One of the guests really got his attention. I'd started a chapter at Shaw of the 21st Century Youth Leadership Movement and taken a group of students to a training camp at Stillman College in Tuscaloosa, Alabama. There, I met a young woman named Gay Williams Mack and told her about my desire to bring role models into my class to inspire my students. Her husband suggested that she invite her uncle, and I agreed, not knowing who her uncle was.

It turned out he was General Colin Powell, at that time the national security advisor for President Ronald Reagan. He'd later become chairman of the Joint Chiefs of Staff and secretary of state. When I told Dr. Ellis that Gen. Powell was coming to my class, he did not respond at first. Maybe he did not believe me. But when Gen. Powell's advance person called the school, suddenly he became very interested and called me to his office. He wanted to know why Powell was speaking only to my class and not to the entire school. Looking him squarely in the eye, I told him Gen. Powell was there for my students, and they could not come to the auditorium for programs. He said this was too important an event for just one class.

I agreed. I told him all students should be allowed in the auditorium, including those in the White House and Special Ed. In other words, all students had to be able to attend, or it was going to be in my classroom. I knew he didn't like it, but Dr. Ellis agreed to let all students attend. It was a victory for all the students and the teachers who'd been excluded. The program went so well, Gen. Powell stayed far longer than he had originally planned. My class and others who had been outcast were seated right up front. They were so well behaved that they could no longer be exiled. They felt special, and all my students went from being labeled failures to being among the most successful in the school.

After Gen. Powell's visit, I was called back into the office for a meeting. This time, Dr. Ellis was there with Nellie Cook, who taught high-achieving students. I had never been in a meeting with her, and we seldom worked together. Ellis told me that the whole school system was talking about Powell's visit. He praised me for bringing him there. However, he had problems with the student I chose to introduce the general. He said that the student was overweight and did not speak well. So from now on, one of Mrs. Cook's students would introduce any guests I brought to the school. I was appalled, but I managed to say politely that my students would continue to introduce my guests. Needless to say, I became Dr. Ellis's least favorite person that day.

After two years at Shaw, I filed a complaint with the union

over the unfair treatment of teachers and students and was transferred to Kelly Miller Junior High School in Northeast DC. The atmosphere there was very different, with traditional self-contained classrooms. My principal, Ronald Hasty, was a Mississippi native who had learned about my unorthodox way of teaching and welcomed my innovative approach. There were more books, and I had more parental support.

As incentives and for exposure to new experiences, I organized student trips to events in DC. We even went to New York City to visit the famous Apollo Theater in Harlem. One of my friends was an associate producer on *Showtime at the Apollo*. The prospect of earning a coveted seat on the bus to see the taping of the show was a wonderful way to keep the students focused on their tasks. Once again, I started a chapter of the 21st Century Youth Leadership Movement.

Washington, DC, had become known as the murder capital of the United States. Kelly Miller, located next to Lincoln Heights, a public housing complex, saw more than its share of violence. One day a helicopter landed on our playground to pick up a victim who had been shot in Lincoln Heights. Another time a parent-teacher conference was interrupted when one of our students was mistakenly identified as an assailant who had killed someone in Lincoln Heights.

My students needed hope amid the despair. I decided to take them to Selma for the twenty-fifth anniversary of the Selma to Montgomery march. To prepare, I taught them about the significance of the march. We watched the PBS series *Eyes on the Prize*, and I made study sheets for each episode and tests on the content. Then we had to raise money. Students, now armed with knowledge, became the spokespersons for our fundraising drive. They appeared on a radio show hosted by Dr. Calvin Rolark, founder of the *Washington Informer*, a newspaper that covered the city's Black community. The students and I went to the National Press Building, where Dr. Rolark turned his show into a radiothon to raise money for our trip.

Excitement grew around the city, and people began dropping off checks at the school. The *Washington Post* sent reporter Rene Sanchez to interview us before the trip and to travel to Selma with us. We left in a forty-five-passenger bus full of students, teacher Cynthia Harvey, and three parents.

Traveling to Alabama was an important opportunity for the students, who lived in the midst of senseless violence. On the bus, one eighth grader asked me nonchalantly if I'd ever seen a brain. She then described what she'd seen after a murder. Clearly these students were traumatized, and there was no crisis management team to help them cope. I hoped that learning about their history and gaining inspiration from the stories of others who had faced adversity would help them focus on the future.

Our first major stop was in Atlanta. I took the students to the King Center, and we had breakfast at The Beautiful Restaurant, a well-known soul-food establishment. Our next stop was Tuskegee, where we visited the Carver Museum and toured the campus of Tuskegee University. When we arrived in Selma, a protest was taking place at the city hall. We got off the bus and joined the local demonstrators. At the hotel, we saw visitors from all over the United States, including Jesse Jackson and state and local dignitaries. A busload of students arrived from New York. One of the students in that group, Tarana Burke, went on to become famous for founding the "Me Too" movement against sexual harassment and assault.

Before the march that Sunday, we joined the mass meeting at Brown Chapel AME Church, the starting point for the original marchers in 1965. The students were so excited about finally being able to march across the Edmund Pettus Bridge, and I was as inspired as they were. I realized these were the greatest lessons I could teach them: the value of peaceful protest and the importance of voting to achieve the American dream. They listened to Coretta Scott King, Dick Gregory, and Jesse Jackson, and heard first-person accounts of the original march. The crescendo came when we lined up to cross the bridge with thousands of others. It was a feeling of elation that I had not felt during my first march. My students were finding hope, just as I'd known they would. Rene Sanchez of the *Washington Post* marched beside us, taking down quotes. I felt I was marching with our future, and back home, the nation's capital was cheering us on.

On the second day of the march, the crowd going to Montgomery had narrowed to about three hundred, not unusual considering the distance. My old mentor and friend James Orange was with us every step of the way. Our bus followed along as we walked in case students or parents grew exhausted, and it also provided a place for older marchers to rest or ride along.

One of those older marchers was a woman named Annie Lee Cooper. She was seventy-nine years old, but despite her age and inability to walk long distances, she was determined to be there. She sat at the front of the bus and shared her story the first day through the microphone. It was so moving that she was welcomed on our bus daily. The students affectionately called her "grandmother."

Mrs. Cooper recounted how she had lost her job at Dunn Nursing Home because of her attempts to register to vote and to help others. She had lived in other parts of the country, where she had been able to vote. Yet upon returning to Selma, she was denied that right. Determined to regain it, she began to work with the Dallas County Voters League. Despite appearing demure, one of her claims to fame was that she had knocked down Jim Clark, the notorious sheriff who became synonymous with voter suppression during the height of the voting rights movement in Selma. In the movie *Selma*, she was played by Oprah Winfrey. Mrs. Cooper so endeared herself to the students that many remained in touch with her for years after our trip.

I was asked to choose a student to speak at the capital in Montgomery on the final day of the march, a great honor for us. Lisa Berry, an eighth grader who already exhibited leadership abilities and expressed herself well, was chosen by her peers as the speaker. It was a warm day in March when we arrived triumphantly at the capitol steps. The march had swelled again to thousands. Melba Moore, a Tony Award–winning singer and actress, sang "Lift Every Voice and Sing," often called the Black national anthem. Lisa followed her and gave a rousing five-minute speech. I was very proud of her.

We returned home to cheers from parents and students as the bus turned the corner in front of the school. The local media was there to interview the students, whose eyes gleamed with the realization that they had become symbols of justice in Washington. The accolades for us continued for some time, with honors from the Board of Education and the DC City Council, and an appearance on the *Voice of America*.

My students now had hope.

As a new teacher in DC schools, I had little job security. Being the last hired often meant being the first to be let go or transferred, no matter how successful you were as an educator. Soon my time came, and I was transferred to Eliot Junior High. That experience was very different than what I had experienced at Kelly Miller. The events within the city seemed to touch my students more closely there. Maybe they'd just grown to accept the violence. Also, I had never seen administrators so blatantly state that they did not expect the students to succeed.

Even more appalling, when a student was raped the principal dismissed it as simply "something that these children do." The same school system that applauded me for the Selma trip was now failing to protect a student who was clearly a victim. They attempted to cover up what happened and what they knew.

It became even stranger when I was asked to appear on a radio show and be interviewed by G. Gordon Liddy, the former Nixon operative and Watergate burglar, after I spoke out about the rape. I'd talked to the victim's parents and the police and joined the parents in a lawsuit against the school system, challenging its inaction. As a result, I was being harassed by administrators who had looked the other way. I'd received threats, and Liddy, a former FBI agent, offered to help me if I had issues with security. Friends and associates asked me why I sought to help the student who was the victim in this case. Clearly jobs trumped values, and folks were willing to look the other way if the child was not one of privilege.

I knew that my time in DC was coming to an end. My experience at Kelly Miller was awesome, but I'd witnessed a lot of suffering endured by students. Many had seen dead bodies, and trauma was becoming all too common. The convergence of events convinced me I would not be able to raise a child in that city. I longed for a rural setting in a community more aligned with my values.

Thurgood was from Raeford, North Carolina, and during the turmoil in DC we received a call that his father had suffered a stroke. After visiting him in the hospital, we decided it was time to move to North Carolina to help. Thurgood's memory had returned after several months, but he still suffered from bad headaches. Despite his disability, he had returned to school and earned a degree in family counseling at the University of the District of Columbia, but he was never able to fully go back into the workforce. Teaching allowed me the flexibility to move, since I could teach anywhere.

We decided to live in Fayetteville, near Raeford, and to become parents. Our daughter, Taylor, was born in North Carolina, and I pictured a different kind of life. I thought that once I became a mother, I would leave the justice suit in the closet for a while. I wasn't expecting to take up any new causes, but of course nothing went as planned.

I became a teacher at Hoke High School, the same high school that Thurgood had attended, in the school system where his mother had been an administrator. Thurgood's family was exceptional in many ways and was well known in the community. That was evident when I interviewed with the assistant superintendent, who was the highest-ranking Black person in the administration. She made a point of telling me that she'd had many dinners at my in-laws' home.

I'd married into a family of strong women. Thurgood's mother, Nellie, had completed her master's degree in education at Columbia University, and her sisters were all accomplished. Phloy, who lived next door, was among the first fifty-six Black nurses admitted to the U.S. Army Nurses Corps in 1941. I'd never known that Black women served as officers in World War II until I saw a picture of her in uniform with bars on her shoulder. Pearl lived in Washington, DC, and was retired from the Justice Department. Mamie, a former nurse who lived in Tuskegee, was the widow of a Tuskegee airman. Alice lived in Haverstraw, New York, by the Hudson River. She retired as a supervisor at Letchworth State Village and belonged to the NAACP.

My father-in-law, Robert, was a World War II veteran who had retired from his job as a cook at a nearby state prison and owned a septic tank cleaning business. Nellie's brother, affectionately called Uncle Buddy, had worked in construction before his arthritis forced him to retire.

I felt happy to be a part of this amazing clan.

At Hoke High I taught Current Events, U.S. History, and Street Law, a program I'd learned about on my first trip to DC. The concept originated at Georgetown School of Law in 1972, with law students going to secondary schools to teach the basics of law and government. At that time, the U.S. Supreme Court had ruled that a student could not be suspended from school without a hearing, and student rights were a big issue. When I returned to DC to teach in 1992, I reconnected with administrators of the project, which had become known simply as Street Law and spread to other cities.

Soon after I arrived, I started planning another field trip. It was an election year, and Bill Clinton, Ross Perot, and the incumbent, George H.W. Bush, were in the running. When I interviewed to work for the school system, I said I'd like to take students to the inauguration, no matter who the winner was, and after I got the job I was determined to follow through.

Even though it was billed as "the people's inauguration," I had a hard time getting information about the events as I was simply a teacher, not a big donor or elected official. I was going to have to take extreme measures. On my Christmas break, I went to Washington to volunteer with the Clinton Inaugural Committee, and was placed in the office that assisted the first lady's family. I answered phones there a few days, and then I was invited to be a hostess at the Arkansas Ball, one of several balls. It was a coveted invitation. I asked if my husband could volunteer as well, and the answer was yes.

As promised, I took a busload of students and chaperones to Washington for all the public events. The experience endeared me to a lot of students and parents. I was a new teacher giving them a chance to experience history. I had booked a hotel and found a bus company that would provide transportation to Washington and then take us around the city. Everyone—parents, students, and chaperones—was involved in raising money with car washes and fish fries. The students were very excited.

Once we'd seen President Clinton sworn in and some of the sights, it was time to get ready for the ball. I changed into a long black gown, and Thurgood put on a tuxedo, and we headed to the Arkansas Ball. We were assigned to be a host and hostess, and my job was to answer questions and assist special guests in an area set up for television interviews. I saw actor Billy Baldwin in a tux and sneakers and watched Katie Couric conduct interviews. As I stood marveling at the beautiful gowns women were wearing, a very handsome man leaned down and asked me how to get to where Barbra Streisand was being interviewed. It was Peter Jennings. I still remember his breath smelled like mints.

A teenage Chelsea Clinton would sometimes dart in and out with her friends in tow. I saw Dionne Warwick sitting alone in the dressing room, but I didn't approach her. She seemed to want some quiet time. The highlight of the evening was Clarence Clemons of the E Street Band giving Bill Clinton his saxophone to blow a few notes.

Back at school, I was beginning to get to know my students better. I always had an open-door policy, encouraging students to talk to me. They began opening up, telling me about unequal treatment at the high school. For example, Black students felt they could never be valedictorians or salutatorians of their senior class, because they were limited in their ability to take advanced placement classes. They had to be recommended by one of the instructors teaching the classes. All the instructors were white, and they seldom recommended students of color.

The inequities were not immediately evident to me, but several events made them impossible to ignore. An annual pageant known as Miss Ekoh—Hoke spelled backward—crowned a Black queen on a Friday night. By Monday, it was announced that the votes were miscalculated, and her crown was removed. A policy was enacted to allow school officials to enter classes and search students with cause. Several students were suspended because they had knives. One of them was a white honor student. There was an uproar in the media about the white student's suspension, but no clamor about the Black students involved.

I noticed that white seniors knew by the end of the first semester which university they would enter upon graduation. Many of the Black students had not even completed financial aid applications, because the guidance counselors ignored them and their needs. It became increasingly clear that there was a hierarchy based on race and privilege. At the top were upper-middle-class white students. In the second tier were poor and middle-class white students. The third tier was for Black students. At the bottom of the hierarchy were indigenous students, known as the Lumbee. The divisions harkened back to the days of segregation, when white, Black, and Indian students went to separate schools.

The Lumbee are the largest tribe recognized in North Carolina, and if they received full federal recognition, they would become the largest tribe east of the Mississippi River. They were also the third largest group of students at Hoke High. One day one of my female students told me she was Lumbee. I had never wondered about her ancestry, but I had assumed that she was bi-racial. I had noticed the red hair and gray eyes of many of the students. Some even spoke with a different accent. I later discovered they were from a part of the county called South Hoke, which had a large population of Lumbee.

The teacher became the student. The young lady, whom I will call Valerie, shared stories of folk heroes like Henry Berry Lowry, who led guerilla attacks on Confederate troops during the Civil War and stole from upper-class white people to give to the poor. She also told me about celebrations of her culture called powwows. She introduced me to other indigenous students, including one named Tuskaloosa, whose name interested me because Tuscaloosa is a city in Alabama. Tuskaloosa was a senior who wore his hair long and was indeed proud of his culture. He seemed wise beyond his years and was a natural leader. During our first discussion, he told me that he was a Tuscarora Indian and his father had been a member of the American Indian Movement, which had developed alongside the civil rights movement to procure sovereignty rights for indigenous peoples.

Valerie told me there were no activities at the school acknowledging their heritage, which predated the colonization of what is now North Carolina. She asked if I would sponsor a powwow at the school, and I agreed. I met with Tuskaloosa's father, and he got parents involved. Convincing school officials to go along took some politicking, but with the help of the parents and local Lumbee leaders, the powwow became a reality.

It was held in the gym during the school day and was well attended, with ceremonies, dances, drumming, and oral histories. Tuskaloosa, speaking in melodic tones, shared a story of the history of his people that had the students mesmerized. The powwow was an important cultural experience that helped all students gain more knowledge and respect for the Lumbee. A Lumbee parent who was an artisan thanked me with a dream catcher for my baby daughter and a choker for me to wear. Parents wrote letters of gratitude. That first conversation with Valerie had opened a new world to me, something I still appreciate to this day.

My Street Law and Current Events classes were very popular, especially when I invited the state director of the American Civil Liberties Union to speak to my students. Interest was so great that we had to meet in the library so other teachers could bring their classes. Students listened, asked questions, and described scenarios in which they felt their rights had been violated by school officials and law enforcement. For example, police would search the cars of students leaving the parking lot after school. Students also complained of being searched in class without a reason. According to our speaker, many of these actions were legally questionable.

Afterward, some teachers complained that I was teaching students how to break the law. I saw it differently. I knew first-hand of many violations of Title VI of the Civil Rights Act of 1964, which prohibits discrimination in schools. I wasn't going to tolerate unjust treatment of young people, and I decided to act. Applying what I had learned during my high school days in Lowndes County, I began documenting the violations. Then I filed a complaint with the U.S. Department of Education Office of Civil Rights against the Hoke County School Board.

This was serious. If the complaint was found credible, the school system would have to agree to correct the wrongs or lose federal money. The Office of Civil Rights found my allegations compelling enough to send an investigator to look into them. His presence must have sent shivers through the administration and the school board, and it became known that I was the person filing the complaint.

Racism was so ingrained in the system that the documents the board provided in response to the complaint proved my allegations. Discriminatory behavior was so commonplace and freely documented, it appeared administrators did not know or care that it was illegal.

I got permission from my husband's Uncle Buddy to hold

a public meeting at Rock Hill Missionary Baptist Church, where he was chairman of the deacons. He supported what I was doing, even though he knew his sister, my mother-in-law, might not feel comfortable about it. At the meeting, members of the community gave the investigator even more information about their experience with racist practices by the school board.

Of course, the complaint made me very unpopular among some of the teachers, counselors, and administrators. The harassment started. Again I was accused of teaching the students to break the law. One teacher said I was making the other teachers look bad. Then a Black student was killed in a senseless shooting. Before it happened, he had told me he'd been at a club when gunfire broke out and five people were killed; he said he had no part in it and feared for his life. Now he was a victim, gunned down while standing in his girlfriend's front yard. I heard rumors that his death was driven by revenge over the earlier shootings where he'd been present.

After his death, his friends told me about a heartbreaking situation. They said his mother was white, a loner in the community who did not know many people. She was staying at the funeral home with her son's body every night until the funeral. She had originally planned to hold the services in the funeral home, but his friends were hoping for a bigger place so they could all celebrate his life with her. They asked me to talk with her, and I did. She agreed, but needed help finding a location. I went to one of the principals to ask if she could use the auditorium at a school building. We struck a deal that she could use an auditorium for free. But after the administration discovered I had filed the civil rights complaint, I received a bill for the funeral. They took the money out of my meager paycheck.

I was accustomed to living under pressure, but this time it

hit close to home. One of the blows came when my mother-in-law asked me to drop by to see her. She asked who had given me permission to hold the meeting at the church. Reluctantly, I said it was her brother, Uncle Buddy. She expressed her dismay, saying that the people being investigated were her friends. She was a good Christian woman, and I appealed to her faith. I said that as a teacher and a Christian, I was bound by my faith and profession to provide equal access to educational opportunities for all students. I questioned how we as Christians could justify not trying to change inequities. I knew she had a deep respect for justice and fairness. It was in her DNA. But she stuck to her position and did not waver.

I didn't understand her pushback at the time, but later I realized that what she exhibited was a survival mechanism. She had survived all these years by working hard and not rocking the boat, even though she herself was a victim of discrimination. Despite her advanced degree from a prestigious university, her wages were based on a Jim Crow pay scale. White administrators were paid more.

Ultimately, the Office of Civil Rights found that school discipline of students was clearly race-based. Suspension rates among students of color were disproportionately high, especially for indigenous students, whose suspension rates were the highest of all. Counselors did not provide students of color the same guidance that they offered white students, and their advice was sometimes ill informed. For example, when a Black female student was offered a scholarship to Spelman College, one of the most distinguished historically Black institutions, her white counselor told her that Spelman was not a good school.

The district had to negotiate an agreement with the Office of Civil Rights stating how the issues would be remedied. I was involved in the negotiations and had to sign off on the agreement. It called for high school administrators to follow a fourteen-point plan, including training teachers on issues of sensitivity and cultural awareness. They would condone ethnic attire, design an African American history course, and stop considering race and gender in applications for advanced placement classes. Later, I was told that I was the first teacher in the history of the U.S. Department of Education to file a federal civil rights complaint on behalf of students.

I'd succeeded in helping the students, but at a cost. I had come to a close-knit community and upset the status quo. The stress was more than I'd expected. Migraines, which I'd begun having when I was in the military, became more frequent. Once again, I was ready to move.

I'd learned that Detroit schools had an African-centered curriculum, and I was excited about the possibility of working there. We started making plans to move to Detroit as a family, but in the end, Thurgood chose to stay with his family. Taylor and I went without him.

Before I had a chance to find a teaching job in Detroit, my plans changed, and I took a brief detour. The Southern Christian Leadership Conference was holding its national convention in Detroit, with well-known civil rights leaders attending from around the nation. SCLC was like family to me, so I decided to go. The first day, I ran into attorney Rose Sanders, my old friend and mentor from Selma.

Rose and I had kept in touch over the years. She was a founder of the 21st Century Youth Leadership Movement, and I had started chapters of the program at every school where I was employed. Now she approached me with Martin Luther King III and asked me if I would consider becoming the director of the National Voting Rights Museum in Selma. I said no. The next day when I saw her, she was with Andrew Young. She told him she was trying to convince me to take the museum job. He asked what I did professionally, and I told him I was a teacher. He said this would be an excellent opportunity for me to help the museum. Because of my deep respect for him, I reluctantly accepted the job as the museum's first director and moved to Selma.

I was only there a year before I moved to Detroit, but a couple of highlights stand out, partly because they led to lasting friendships.

The thirty-second anniversary of Bloody Sunday and the Selma to Montgomery march was coming up, and I enjoyed planning events for the celebration around the march, now called the Jubilee. My friend Sheila Frazier, best known for co-starring in the movie *Super Fly*, was heading the talent department at BET, and she worked with me as talent coordinator. She was able to get attorney Johnnie Cochran, singers Tramaine Hawkins and Howard Hewett, and Malcolm X's daughter, writer Attallah Shabazz, as headliners.

Also, I attended the signing of the agreement to build the first interpretive center along the Selma to Montgomery March Trail in Lowndes County. The Lowndes Interpretive Center houses exhibits that tell about the march and describe the struggles of Black Lowndes County residents at the time. The ceremony took place in the old Executive Office Building of the White House, and it was my first time meeting then Vice President Al Gore, who would become an important person in my life.

My time in Detroit turned out to be one of the best experiences in my teaching career. I started off at Phoenix Multicultural Academy and planned to stay there. But after I conducted a workshop for history teachers about motivating students, I was offered a coveted position at Renaissance High School.

Renaissance was a magnet school where more than 90 percent of students received college scholarships. Parents came to meetings with calculators to keep up with their children's progress, and they were very supportive of any efforts to expose their children to various settings. I felt torn about leaving Phoenix so soon, but teachers waited years to work at Renaissance. I couldn't pass up the opportunity.

Students at Renaissance were very talented and seriously concerned about the world around them. They would often ask me why I was teaching instead of running for office. Some even compared me to Oprah, I guess because I had lively class discussions where everyone felt free to express their opinion. I encouraged my students, who knew many influencers in the city, to invite guest speakers, and they did. A great class is one where the students are engaged, not sitting quietly at their desks every day, copying work written on a board. Our classes were great by that measure.

I created lessons around intergenerational projects. When the students interviewed their parents and grandparents about the march on Washington and the Detroit riots, their writings were so impressive they were included in an anthology about Detroit's history.

The thirty-fifth anniversary of the original Selma to Montgomery march was coming up, and I decided to take Renaissance students there. It would be a big feat to raise enough money to ensure that students who could not afford the trip could still go. The parents were excited and enlisted help from all sectors of the city. One parent, a police officer, invited me to a meeting at a union hall of the Coalition of Black Trade Unionists. I walked into the building and immediately noticed a huge picture on the wall of student marchers being beaten in Montgomery. One of the marchers was Willie "Mukasa" Ricks, who'd been a frequent visitor to my parents' home in Lowndes County and coined the phrase "Black power."

I sat facing the group, and the parent who'd invited me asked, "Do you know where you are?" I said I was at a union hall, and that I was surprised to see a picture that I knew so well. He explained, "This hall is named for Nelson Jack Edwards. He was from Lowndes County." I was amazed at the connection. Edwards was born in Lowndes County in 1917 and was run out of the county when the Klan fired into his home. He fled to Detroit, where he became a union organizer and a champion of civil rights. Eventually, he was the first Black vice president of the United Auto Workers.

Edwards was one of many Black people from the South to migrate to the "Motor City" to work in the automobile industry. Many of those transplants and their families became civil rights activists, fighting in Detroit against segregation in the South and elsewhere. So many came from Lowndes County that historians Taylor Branch and Hasan Jeffries asked me for help when they came to Detroit in 2000 to interview people who remembered the struggle back home. Branch was researching his landmark volume *At Canaan's Edge: America in the King Years 1965–68*, which featured Lowndes County prominently, and Hasan Jeffries was researching his dissertation, which later became the book *Bloody Lowndes*. I was able to connect them with people who could give them firsthand accounts.

That connection between Lowndes County and Detroit helped us raise enough money for the trip. All kinds of people, including elected officials, dropped off checks, and we left Detroit amid a mild snowfall and a flurry of media attention. The excitement reminded me of the trip I had taken ten years earlier with students from Washington, DC. This time, Dr. Lowery had retired, and Martin Luther King III was leading the march. Comedian and activist Dick Gregory was there all the way. Each day, he and other leaders would stop along the route for speaking engagements, and Gregory would take a few of my students with him. Adults marveled at my students' grasp of the issues, and the media sought them out. I was very proud.

From Highway 80, Lowndes County looked the same as I remembered it. Local people joined us as we walked through their communities. When we stopped for a break at a fire station, a car pulled up, and a familiar face emerged. It was Miss Shug, my childhood neighbor. She had seen me on the news and wanted to deliver a message. "Things are worse for us than they have ever been," she said after she hugged me tightly. "You should come back and help us." Her words weighed on me heavily and resounded in my mind long after she left me.

My parents came the last day of the march. We were at Dexter Avenue Baptist Church in Montgomery, and I noticed that my father was unsteady and shaking a little. He said I should consider returning home. I thought about what Miss Shug had said, and my heart was shattered seeing how fragile my father was. My parents posed for a picture outside the church with Martin Luther King III, Reverend Al Sharpton, and Jock Smith. I hugged them and boarded the bus for the return trip.

Three weeks later, my brother called to tell me my father had suffered a stroke and was in grave condition.

He passed away March 28, 2000. It was at his funeral that I really understood what he meant to our community. I saw men wearing suits whom I had never seen in suits before. The church was full. It helped me to understand the level of respect people had for my father. As an example of his impact, the first person to pay his respects at the funeral home and sign the book was District Judge Ted Bozeman, a longtime white power broker in Lowndes County.

People continued to urge me to come back home, and finally I agreed.

It was time.

Chapter 6

I saw glimmers of hope in the Lowndes County I returned to in 2000. Some Black-owned businesses were succeeding, and their owners were learning how to wield political and economic power. Throughout the county, Black officials had been elected to critical positions, serving as mayors, county commissioners, and school board members. One of my friends from ASU was the newly appointed superintendent of schools.

A multi-racial group had formed to reverse a decision to build a landfill that would accept garbage from other counties. It was a classic example of treating a poor county as a dumping ground. One of the group's leaders was civil rights leader Bob Mants, who used to visit my parents when I was a child. He'd called me several times when I was still in Detroit to discuss strategy. It was one of the first times I could recall residents organizing around an environmental justice issue in Lowndes County.

I hoped to help the people of the county get the services they needed, and also to help bring in economic development. I wasn't sure how, but I had to figure out a way to use my skills and contacts to help propel the area into the twenty-first century. The timing of my return provided a temporary answer. The year 2000 was an election year of both national and local importance. The NAACP asked me to head its Voter Empowerment Office in Selma, and I accepted. I'd be responsible for coordinating nonpartisan efforts to increase voter turnout in Alabama's Black Belt, including a voter registration drive and a massive get-out-the-vote effort.

In Selma, just across the Lowndes County line in Dallas County, voters were working to elect their first Black mayor, James Perkins Jr. He was headed to a September runoff with the nine-term incumbent, Joseph Smitherman. Smitherman had been mayor during the height of the voting rights movement in Selma, and a victory by a Black candidate would carry tremendous emotional and historic weight. We also hoped it would propel voters to return to the polls in massive numbers in November to vote for Al Gore over George W. Bush.

As we hoped, Perkins won in the September 2000 runoff, and it was a joyous occasion. Civil rights leaders came from around the nation on election day, underscoring the significance of the moment. As we celebrated, I was filled with optimism that the tide of change might also bring opportunity for Lowndes County. But first, there was a presidential election in November.

After Perkins's win, excitement was high in Selma and throughout the Black Belt around the presidential election. We coordinated with efforts throughout the state to get voters to the polls, paying special attention to precincts with considerable numbers of Black voters. Both during and after the city elections in Selma, we received threats in the Voter Empowerment Office, and a security guard was detailed to protect our office. Coming from Lowndes County, and with my background in social justice work, I wasn't really surprised. Threats come with the territory.

For years I'd taught students about how the democratic process works. The presidential election provided a lesson in real time when Gore won the popular vote but narrowly lost the electoral vote. It took weeks and a controversial Supreme Court ruling over Florida's ballots before the outcome was finally decided. During that time, one of the Bush camp's supporters who appeared in the media was a Black man named Bob Woodson.

Woodson, a conservative, was a strong advocate for communities in despair, and he'd won a MacArthur "Genius" award for his work. I'd met him years earlier when I took students from Shaw Junior High in Washington to Stillman College for a 21st Century Youth Leadership Development Conference. Our encounter then didn't go well, as I challenged him over his affiliation with the Republican Party. Little did I realize at the time, but we shared some common values, despite our political differences.

After that first meeting, I made a conscious decision not to allow political differences to limit my ability to talk to people about issues. My intuition told me that we would meet again on a more positive note. Now, watching him on TV, I wondered if the time for that meeting had come. I still wasn't sure what my role in Lowndes County would be, but I was committed to helping people like Miss Shug. I had always voted Democratic, but somehow I knew Woodson would be the person to help me.

My work with the NAACP Voter Empowerment Project ended a few months after the general election. I had engaged in many discussions with Charlie King, who was on the Lowndes County Commission (and was also my cousin), about the county's needs. Charlie asked me to consider becoming the economic development consultant for Lowndes County. I submitted a proposal that was approved by the county commission, and my work on behalf of Lowndes County began.

I hadn't been on the job long when I received an invitation to a faith-based summit in Washington, DC. One of the organizers was Elroy Sailor, whom I'd met in Detroit when I'd organized a candidates' night for parents of students at Renaissance High School. Sailor then was an aide to Michigan's Republican governor, John Engler, and attended our event on the governor's behalf. Since then, he'd joined the staff of Representative J.C. Watts of Oklahoma. Watts was one of the hosts of the faith-based summit.

I could not afford to attend the event. I mentioned it to one of my confidantes, Reverend James Nuckles, who was both pastor of my brother's church and a Montgomery City Council member. He told me that he wanted me to go, and he provided funding for lodging and for my brother to drive me to Washington. He could not have known that his action would change the course of my work in Lowndes County, but it did.

I went to Washington not knowing what to expect but praying for help. The summit turned out to be like a convention of ministers and evangelists, with hundreds in attendance. Many of the television ministers were there, dressed in their Sunday best, as were members of Congress from both sides of the aisle. It was well organized, with a series of workshops. I attended an informative workshop conducted by Bishop T.D. Jakes, pastor of a Dallas mega-church, and had a chance to ask him about his church's model for economic development work. He graciously responded and put me in touch with his economic development director.

I attended the luncheon where Bob Woodson was the featured speaker. The room was full of significant faith leaders, and I was not sure if this was my opportunity to approach him. I do not recall what he said that day, but it must have encouraged me, because I followed him after he left the stage and introduced myself. Without flinching, I recounted how our first meeting had not gone well. Then I said, "I am from Lowndes County, Alabama, a poor rural community. We need your help to uplift our community." He gave me his card and asked me to call his secretary and make an appointment to see him.

I went back to Alabama, happy to have made his acquaintance, and set up the appointment. Shortly after September 11, 2001, I flew back to Washington, this time with a delegation from Lowndes County. The trauma of 9/11 hung heavy over the city. Downtown DC seemed almost like a ghost town, and smoke was still drifting from the Pentagon, days after terrorists had crashed a plane into the massive building. I was shaken by what I saw. When Woodson received us, he seemed impressed that we were unafraid to make the trip.

Woodson was a striking figure, tall and debonair, yet attentive and sincerely interested in what we had to say. He was a mixture of Philly cool and DC savvy. He was sympathetic and open to us. Our delegation consisted of former and current county elected officials, including Charlie King, Karl Bell, and Helenor Bell. We described the lack of sustainable economic development in Lowndes County and asked for help transforming the current state of neglect to a future of prosperity. The meeting concluded with Woodson's agreeing to come for a visit.

Meanwhile, I had made several other trips to Washington, Atlanta, and Montgomery, seeking help. The meetings in DC were mostly promising, but nothing happened afterward. One meeting ended with an official from the U.S. Economic Development Administration chuckling as he told me the only reason to go to Lowndes County was to get to Selma or Montgomery. I began to recognize that rural bias was real. It was clear that rural people lacked pull when it came to influencing policy or obtaining federal or state funding. We could not afford a lobbyist, so I felt we needed a prominent politician to champion us.

Alabama senators typically hold town hall meetings to update their constituents about what's going on in Washington and to take questions from local folk. I saw that Senator Jeff Sessions, an Alabama Republican, was holding a town hall meeting in the small Lowndes County town of Fort Deposit. I attended, sitting in the auditorium of the National Guard Armory, and listened carefully as Sessions outlined his efforts to help rural communities. He talked about grants that were available through various federal agencies. He asked if there were any questions. Other than elected officials, I was one of a few Black people in the audience in this majority-Black county and town, but I raised my hand. I thanked him for his presentation and asked about a daunting problem: "How can poor counties with no tax base gain access to funding through grants when a 25 percent match is required?"

For a moment, he was quiet. Then he responded carefully: "You are right. That is a question that I have often thought about." He did not answer my question, but after his presentation, he walked to where I was seated and said, "I grew up poor in Wilcox County. I have often thought about how to get funds to rural areas with no tax base. Would you help me find a way?" I thought it was interesting that he sought to identify with rural issues, and I felt that maybe we could work together.

While waiting for Woodson's visit, I decided to take a bold step. Huddling with some of my friends and influencers in Lowndes, I tossed around the idea of having a fundraiser for one of Alabama's U.S. senators at the home of a county family. Kevin Lawrence, a local businessman, decided to host it. I met with Chuck Spurlock, Sessions's state political director, and he was intrigued by the idea. It would be an opportunity for local businesspeople to discuss problems and solutions. Chuck agreed to do it.

On the day of the fundraiser, Sessions visited a farm in Lowndes County where Lee Jackson was growing shrimp in an inland saltwater pond. The saltwater was a remnant of a prehistoric sea, and remains of ancient aquatic life have been found in the area. Many people from outside the county made the journey that day to see this firsthand, and we were all treated to shrimp from the harvest. After his tour of the farm, Sessions rode with me to the fundraiser. On the way there, he asked how he could help me. I asked him to help Lowndes County. He nodded in response.

The fundraiser was a success because it opened a dialogue between Sessions's office and Black business and political leaders in Lowndes County. It was also the beginning of my access to his office and staff. Woodson's trip provided another political inroad, and the two conservatives became allies on our behalf.

The day finally arrived for Woodson's visit. We gave him a tour of dilapidated homes and took him to a school that was heated by a coal-fired furnace. Students and teachers were often out sick because of the ash lining the building's walls. But it was the trip to the McMeans family homes that changed everything. It was the beginning of my education about raw sewage in Lowndes County and beyond. I think it also sealed Woodson's commitment to work with us. He was appalled by the economic neglect and rural despair he saw.

Bill Raspberry's article in the *Washington Post* served notice to officials in Alabama that others were watching. There was an outcry about the arrests of poor people who could not afford sanitation. With Woodson's help, we put together a coalition of business and community leaders, both local and from throughout the United States, to work on solutions. They had diverse political views, but believed that Lowndes County should not be left behind. Members included Greg Snyder, a senior vice president at HSBC Bank; David Rigby, an engineer; Joe Dudley of Dudley Products; Noel Khalil, a real estate developer, and Terence Mathis, his vice president; and a host of others who came in and out.

Locally, we hosted five town hall meetings to learn about the problems families faced. The first meeting took place at the old white-frame Ramer Baptist Church in Calhoun. Voices echoed to the rafters as people filled the two rows of simple wooden pews. Some men were still covered with dust as if they'd come straight from the fields.

The meeting was scheduled to begin at 6:00 p.m., but the church was full by 5:30. People were eager to share their frustrations about failing septic tanks, no septic tanks, and high electric bills. Speakers were not selected beforehand, so we didn't know what to expect. But they came forward to tell their stories as if they had been waiting a long time for this moment. Young and old told of paying high rates for poor services and trying to survive under the weight of poverty, low-wage jobs, and financial exploitation. It was a deeply emotional evening, and tears flowed as speakers shared their pain. We all felt it.

There is a widely accepted narrative that poor people aren't willing to lift themselves by their bootstraps. Anyone attending that meeting would have known otherwise. These were hard-working people, but their efforts to survive and to escape poverty were hindered by rural bias and preconceived notions among public officials and others. It was a matter of inequality, including unequal access to sanitation.

Woodson embarked on a broad program to help us. First, he organized the Alabama Rural Initiative and hired me as its director. The organization later became the Alabama Center for Rural Enterprise, a variation of his National Center for Neighborhood Enterprise. He brought in several partners to help us craft a plan. One of the partners was Clifton Henry, a self-described yellow-dog Democrat and Woodson's best friend. As a youth, Cliff had been a member of SNCC and was active in the movement to desegregate the eastern shore of Maryland. He was an authority on economic development, with a professional practice that focused on market, economic, and financial feasibility analyses for housing, shopping centers, museums, and downtown mixed-use projects around the country. He helped me develop a comprehensive economic development plan for Lowndes County.

Meanwhile, numerous residents still faced arrest for lacking wastewater treatment. Fortunately, Bill Raspberry's article continued to produce ripple effects. It caught the attention of Ron Pugh, the local environmentalist for the state health department. Impressed by the piece, he offered his help. There was only so much he could do, but I welcomed the gesture. I invited him to attend one of our community meetings and explain his role, and he accepted.

As I introduced him to the audience, some began to boo. He was the person issuing citations for failing or nonexistent septic systems, and was seen as the enemy. He tried to explain the purpose of a perc test, which determines how well soil will absorb water, a major factor in issuing permits for septic tanks. Perc tests are mandatory and can cost $600, a heavy expense for people barely earning a living wage. Some in the audience felt perc testing was another way to gouge poor people for more money. He left the church before the meeting ended because he feared that it would not be safe for him to remain.

He invited me to meet him at his office, and I accepted. He met me in the reception area with a smile and invited me to come to the rear of the building where his desk and files were.

He explained how the data were in disarray when he got there, and said there was no real record of how many people had permitted systems. He said he did not want to prosecute people, but his job demanded it. Then he explained how the system worked from his perspective.

The septic problem was so widespread that the health department acted only when it received a complaint. He understood that many of the people cited were poor, and said he only acted after giving them time to correct the problem. I asked Pugh how people in a poor area could come up in a few months with more money than most made in a year. He just shook his head. He understood.

While we were talking, a local builder, who was Black, came into his office. He wanted to see if a woman named Margaree Aaron in his area had a permitted septic system. If not, he was going to help her apply for a grant to get the system since she was a senior citizen. A check of the records found no permit on file.

After the builder left, Pugh asked me to ride with him to see some of the areas that were plagued by raw sewage. We drove to a cluster of trailers where the grass was much greener in one part of the yard than the rest. "This is how you can tell there is either no septic system or a failed septic system there," Pugh said.

We went to a few more sites before Pugh pulled off the main road onto a lot where a small house sat. As we followed a path to the back of the house, he said this was Margaree Aaron's home, the house that the builder had come into his office to discuss. It was evident that the elderly woman's septic tank was not working. Feces clung to the back of her home outside the bathroom. It dawned on me that the builder had reported the woman to the health department under the guise of seeking ways to help her. She could have received a citation and eventually been arrested for not being able to afford a septic system. If she did manage to acquire one, the builder would benefit.

I realized then that an economy had evolved that preyed on impoverished citizens with the help of the state health department. I don't know if Pugh intended for me to see this, but I think he might have. I believe he was a man of conscience. And what happened next showed me that he realized the state's approach was yielding more victims than solutions.

A few days later, he called and asked if I would go to court with him the following day. A young man who lived with his wife and child had been cited for not having a septic tank and was in danger of going to jail for up to ninety days and losing his job. He had even bought a septic tank but didn't have the $6,000 he would need to install it. At that time, he was one of thirty-seven homeowners who had been cited. Pugh wanted me to tell the judge about my efforts to address the problem, hoping she would have mercy on the young man.

Immediately, I called Bob Woodson. He arranged a call in the morning with an array of lawyers, business leaders, and Armand DeKeyser, who was Jeff Sessions's chief of staff. Armand and his staff had researched the Lowndes County arrests and found the judge was holding people in contempt of court on the grounds that they had disobeyed an order to fix their septic systems or to purchase new ones. At least a dozen had been arrested. The lawyers on the call chimed in and gave me my marching orders. Then I left for the Lowndes County courthouse.

The courthouse sits at one end of the town square in the center of Hayneville. It's the same square where I took my first driving test and parallel parked for the first time. Across from the courthouse in the center of the square is a memorial to veterans of the Civil War. It's a tribute not to the United

States, but to the Confederate States of America. Ironically, many of the last names on the memorial are the family names of Lowndes County's Black residents. It serves as a constant reminder of the history of enslavement there and throughout the state. The memorial's location in clear view of the court-house struck me as an ominous statement about justice in a county that is predominantly African American. It seemed to be a warning of our "place" in this society.

When I walked into the courtroom, the young man, Antonio Hinson, was sitting silently at the defense table. The judge who had ordered the residents' arrests was presiding in her robe. A bailiff sat to her right. Pugh asked if he could approach the bench with me. Pugh introduced me as the person who was seeking to help address the raw sewage issue and asked that I be allowed to speak on behalf of the defendant. The judge scowled at me and said, "I am getting calls from around the country accusing me of putting poor people in jail." I realized this was no time to be intimidated. I needed to look her in the eye and say what the lawyers had coached me to say.

I told her she was arresting people without an adequate legal foundation. The proper way to address this would be to allow us to find solutions. I was respectful, but firm. Yet it was such a tense moment, and apparently so unexpected, that the bailiff stood up as if he might have to take action.

The exchange reminded me of Freudian theory from one of my counseling classes in graduate school. When the judge spoke to my id, I talked to her ego. It seemed to help. She responded at first with a narrative that I had heard before about how poor people always seem to be able to pay for things they want, like satellite dishes. I don't think she meant to say that out loud. I think she wanted to be fair, but preconceived notions and false ideas colored her judgment.

Calming down a bit, she adjusted her tone. Referring to the

help I was trying to get, she said, "Bring those resources here. We need them." She did not put Antonio in jail, and that was a victory. He was allowed to leave and return to work, much to his relief. A few days later, Woodson came to town to meet the family. We gave them money to get the septic system, and his wife later came to work for us as an office assistant.

In April 2002, Hyundai announced that it was locating its first U.S. plant in Montgomery County. The announcement was exciting because so many people had left the South to work in automobile plants in the North. It raised hopes that good-paying factory jobs could drive a reverse migration to jobs here. It was tremendous news for the Black Belt, where unemployment was high. Governor Don Siegelman, whom I'd known since college, got to confirm the news. Don was a good guy, but rural biases exist regardless of the political party or good intentions of the people running the government. The structures that enable the inequality must change.

Siegelman's office invited me to the groundbreaking ceremony, and I shared that news with the elected officials in Lowndes. On the day of the event, they were calling me to find out the exact location because they had not received official invitations, even though Lowndes County was just a few miles from the plant site. In fact, all the dignitaries with shovels were white people, and the Black Belt counties were mostly left out.

Later, a group of us from Lowndes County met with the governor and Hyundai officials to discuss locating tier-one suppliers in Lowndes County. The meeting resulted in two suppliers' coming there. I wrote the application for the Economic Development Administration grant to finance the infrastructure for two new industrial parks that would host the suppliers, but I was still surprised when the undersecretary for the EDA and Jeff Sessions both gave me credit for helping to bring the plants to Lowndes County. It was a minor victory in our fight to bring jobs to the county. Little did I know that a significant battle over wastewater inequality for residents loomed.

All this time, we'd been negotiating with the state health department over the policy of arresting homeowners with inadequate sewage treatment. Our talks culminated in a meeting that included the state health director, the state environmentalist, representatives from the Alabama Onsite Wastewater Association Training Center, Bob Woodson, and me. Initially, the state health director took a hard line about the wastewater problem, but he ultimately softened his stance, admitting that the problem was so widespread that the department responded only when someone made a complaint.

Besides Woodson and me, there was only one other Black person at the meeting, a staffer from the health department. It seemed extraordinary that the tensest exchanges were between this woman and me. She argued fervently for continued arrests of residents without septic systems, but she lost that battle. When we left the meeting, the consensus was to work on solutions instead of arresting people. Residents previously cited for arrest were to receive help first.

Woodson hired Robert Jones, a former health department employee from Wilcox County, to serve as the project manager for septic tank installations. He had worked as an environmentalist for the region. The consulting engineer was Dr. Kevin White from the University of South Alabama.

Woodson was astute at finding potential funders and bringing them to Lowndes County. One prominent donor, Greg Snyder, was from HSBC bank. With his support, twenty homes received new septic systems or repairs. They were all designed by White and installed by Jones. Most families were happy with the installations and did not complain. However, a few did contact us about problems occurring after installation.

When we questioned the contractors, they responded that the families did not know how to maintain a septic system correctly. We had no reason to believe there were other issues involved, but this was one of the first hints at technology failures that were more complicated than simple maintenance issues.

I continued learning more about soil and sewage treatment, and had some excellent teachers. One was Prest Allender, the state environmentalist. Prest was a graduate of Auburn University in Auburn, Alabama, and often joked they bled orange and blue at his home. We shared rural roots, and he was sincere about finding a long-term solution to the wastewater problem. We had frequent, off-the-record discussions, and Prest shared information to show that the problem was not limited to poor Black communities.

One day, he called and asked me to meet him in Lowndesboro, a small, wealthy community with beautiful homes near Highway 80. We met alongside the county road that went through the town. There, Prest introduced me to a Dr. Albert Rubin, a soil scientist at North Carolina State University. Rubin said he had read about the raw sewage problem in the *New York Times* and had decided to come give me a lesson on soil science and wastewater treatment. He went to a few sites with me to do perc tests and showed how soil varied by location in Lowndes County. Rubin continued to offer me guidance for many years after that. He was the first person to talk to me about wastewater as a reusable or renewable resource.

My political education continued too. I learned the importance of meeting with officials in Washington. Policy and funding access can be the difference between success and failure in rural communities. In 2002, I traveled to DC to tell every member of the Alabama congressional delegation about the raw sewage problem. Heather Humphries, a staffer at Woodson's National Center for Neighborhood Enterprise, accompanied me to office visits on the Hill. Most of the members were Republican, even though voters in the affected areas skew heavily Democratic.

We first stopped at the office of Senator Richard Shelby to seek funding to alleviate the sewage problem. Initially, Shelby's aide—a white woman—was not interested in submitting an appropriations request on our behalf, telling us we had missed the deadline. But when I told her that she would be responsible for explaining why Shelby did nothing to address raw sewage in the poor Alabama county he represented, she reluctantly gave me the form for the request, saying she couldn't make any promises. Whether it was an act of conscience or an act of self-preservation, I don't know. My subsequent meetings with Shelby were always pleasant and supportive. The appropriation made it into the budget, but I had to meet with the rest of Alabama's congressional delegation to keep it there.

One such meeting was in the office of Representative Bob Riley, a Republican who would later serve as Alabama's governor. A staffer said that the congressman might not be able to see us. But I had once worked for Representative Bob Garcia of the South Bronx, so I knew that when guests are taken into a representative's office to wait, usually he or she would appear. That's what happened in Riley's office. After a lengthy conversation, he assured us of his support for the appropriation, and soon all nine members of Alabama's delegation met with us and pledged their support. Our last visit was to the office of then Speaker of the House Dennis Hastert of Illinois. Though we didn't get to speak to him directly, his aide assured us he would support keeping the appropriation request in the budget.

After our appropriation request became part of the 2002 federal budget, we organized the Black Belt Water and Sewer Authority to administer federal funds to repair or install septic tanks in homes where the state health department cited owners. We hired experts, who wrote two work plans for the Environmental Protection Agency to approve. One plan, written by an engineering professor, was turned down as inadequate. The next one was written by a vice president and associate dean of a Jesuit institution who was an expert grant writer and very familiar with developing work plans. His work plan was turned down as too complicated. Finally, I wrote a work plan, and it was approved.

Despite this approval, it would be eight years before we'd see the funds.

Chapter 7

Woodson continued to bring visitors, many of them high profile and influential, to witness the poverty in Lowndes County. These visitors got an education about a way of life they didn't know existed in America. For many, it was their first time even going into a mobile home or a house where families had no running water.

Two televangelists, Reverends Jim Robison and Creflo Dollar, came to visit, and afterward spread the word to their huge audiences about what they had seen. Robison, founder of a relief organization called LIFE Outreach International in Fort Worth, Texas, is co-host of *LIFE Today*, a daily inspirational television program that reaches more than 150 million households in the United States, Canada, Europe, and Australia. Creflo Dollar founded World Changers Church International, headquartered in Georgia. His Changing Your World network is broadcast around the world.

Both found the living conditions they witnessed heart-wrenching. We ended the day at a church, where we worshiped and prayed. Dollar went on to produce a documentary called *A Dream Betrayed* based on his visit, and it won a regional Emmy award. Robison invited me to Dallas to appear on his television show. His wife told me he had trouble sleeping after visiting Lowndes County. He wrote about his experience in this op-ed entitled "The Parable of the Good American":

The Parable of the Good American
    By James Robison
    One day a politician asked, "What does this country have to do to prosper?"
    A wise man replied, "Love your neighbor as yourself."
    The politician said, "And who is my neighbor?"
    The wise man told this story: "A man was living in rural Alabama, trying to care for his family while living in abject poverty. They lived in a rundown trailer, had no sewage system, drank well water and had to drive an hour to work just to make minimum wage. His children went to some of the lowest-ranked public schools in the country. Local law enforcement threatened to throw the man in jail if he didn't install a septic tank, which the man could not afford to do.
    "A reverend happened to be marching through his county. When he saw the man, he passed by on the other side. A senator came to the state and saw him, but he also passed by on the other side. Then an American, just an ordinary guy, went to where the man and his family lived. When he saw them, he took pity on them. He went and helped them, pouring out his sweat and giving of his money. Then he put the man and his family in his own car, took them to a motel and took care of him while the workmen modernized his home. The next day he took out a credit card and gave it to the motel clerk. 'Look after him and his family,' he said, 'and when I return, I will take care of all of their expenses.'

"Which of these three do you think was a neighbor to the poor man in Alabama?

The politician replied, "The one who had mercy on him."

The wise man told him, "Go and do the same thing."

This story is true. The people are real. Many of them live in Lowndes County, which has been dubbed part of the "Third World" of Alabama. The famous Selma-to-Montgomery March runs for over 40 miles through Lowndes County. It has been designated as a National Historic Trail. Numerous re-enactments of the 1965 civil rights march have taken place here. Yet these people do not benefit. They have been completely bypassed. Some have been arrested because they cannot afford to install septic tanks.

The majority of these people are not lazy. They are not drug addicts. They are not welfare junkies. They work hard, love their families, attend church and help each other in a way that is unusual in most middle-class neighborhoods. But they are dirt poor.

The Taylor family has lovingly and faithfully raised their five children in Lowndes County. One son recently served in the Middle East, helping to protect our freedoms and privileges. Mr. Taylor's elderly parents are incapacitated, so he feeds them every day through a tube. This man exemplifies the spirit of America. He is a man of great character. Yet, he and his family seem to be overlooked by society.

I, for one, will not let them be ignored any more. I will help them. I will write columns, speak on television, communicate with our political leaders and support the humanitarian relief financially until something changes. I will seek to be one "Good American." I hope you will, too.

The evangelists were well intended and wanted to model a solution. However, poverty is not easily alleviated when systems are intentionally designed to marginalize people. The systems themselves need to be changed, starting with the lack of political influence wielded by rural counties.

President Richard Nixon's urban affairs advisor Daniel Patrick Moynihan coined the phrase "benign neglect" in 1970 to describe a policy of disinvestment focused on urban Black communities. It was meant to punish urban areas where Black communities rioted to protest discrimination. That policy has since been discredited, but rural America continues to suffer from benign neglect, even though it's not an official government position.

A few weeks before Christmas 2004, Citigroup executives Martin Wong, Mary Louise Preis, and Kevin Kessinger visited Lowndes County with Woodson and Cliff Henry, Woodson's close friend and a respected economic development advisor. The three were members of the senior leadership team at the banking giant. The night before, we had dinner at a barbeque restaurant to get acquainted. I didn't know enough about Citigroup to be intimidated about meeting these folks and was very honest about the issues we were seeking to address.

It was freezing that Saturday morning when we drove to Lowndes County. We had arranged to visit the homes of four families. None had sewage treatment, and all lived in terribly run-down housing. In one home, the family had no running water at all. The second was the home of Margaree Aaron, the older woman whose house I had visited with Ron Pugh from the state health department. Raw sewage still ran under her house. The third visit was with a family that used rags to plug holes to keep rats out of the house. The fourth family paid rent on a shack while the landlord lived in Florida. The mother and her grandchildren huddled in one room to stay warm. A spigot in the backyard provided their water. They'd fill buckets from a hose to carry in the house for drinking, cooking, bathing, and cleaning.

Some members of each household worked but did not earn enough money to change their condition. Young children lived in most of the homes. Obviously, political and economic policies had failed to help these families. By the time we left the last house, our guests were talking about Mother Teresa and the work she was doing in Calcutta. Clearly they were rattled by what they saw, and they took action.

This visit from the Citigroup representatives resulted in all the families' receiving refurbished mobile homes and septic tanks. Two families were relocated because they did not own the land where they lived. Stephanie Wallace, the sister of NBA star Ben Wallace, coordinated the moves. Attorney Randall Bozeman, the brother of the judge I'd encountered earlier, helped prepare legal documents for deeds and titles.

It was a community effort. Volunteers provided clothing, linen, and furniture for the families. McLain, Mississippi, mayor Mary Bolton drove over from Mississippi to help. Tears flowed as the families entered their new homes after the ribbon cuttings. A reporter from the *Birmingham News* interviewed me. Through more tears, I expressed my joy and gratitude for the help donated to these families.

Although we'd made progress in bringing attention to Lowndes County's problems, by 2006 the collaboration with Woodson was coming to an end. The organization we started in Lowndes County as an offshoot of his National Center for Neighborhood Enterprise would continue as the Alabama Center for Rural Enterprise (ACRE), but it was time for me to explore different solutions. We were not always in lockstep in our approach to addressing problems in Lowndes County. Woodson admitted that he was not a rural person, but he tried his best to understand the issues. While our political orientations differed, I found him flexible, willing to learn, and compassionate. His framework for building trust was spot on, and he tried to establish public-private partnerships to arrive at solutions. He had brought influential people and funding to a long-overlooked place and people.

However, we both still had limited knowledge of the raw sewage issue and the extent of it. State health officials focused on residents without septic tanks, but that wasn't the whole story. Even in my parents' house, which had septic tanks, there was a problem with sewage running back into the house. The problem was more complex than installing equipment, and we needed to spend more time understanding it. I was embarking on a different journey, and I'd have to chart my own course.

I was a news junkie like my father. A show I enjoyed watching every Sunday evening was *60 Minutes*. One episode of the program featured attorney Bryan Stevenson and his client, exonerated death-row inmate Walter McMillian. Watching the show, I felt instant admiration for Stevenson's pursuit of justice for McMillian when others had given up hope. As Stevenson investigated and tore through the layers of the case that had led to a death-row sentence for McMillian, he found that his client had been convicted unjustly.

I was beginning to see a similar pattern with the wastewater issue. The facts about the problem, as presented to us by state officials, were not adding up. Those same state officials didn't believe the homeowners, who complained about the technology. It was clear we needed to do a more comprehensive study to determine the extent of the problems and their causes before working on long-term solutions.

One day in 2008, I received a message that someone from Stevenson's organization, the Equal Justice Initiative, wanted to meet me. I immediately returned the call because of my respect for EJI's mission. They were collaborating with Partners in Health, an international social justice organization that brings health care to the world's poorest communities, and were considering opening an office in Lowndes County to offer services there.

We arranged a meeting in White Hall at the ACRE office to see how we could collaborate. During the meeting we discussed raw sewage, poverty, and the range of health conditions we knew existed. I had been told by many of our clients and folks living in the county that they had to choose between buying food and paying for medicine. Many had illnesses such as diabetes and lacked access to healthy foods, since the nearest full-service grocery stores offering fresh fruits and vegetables were in Montgomery, Selma, or Greenville. Instead of taking medications daily as prescribed, many elderly or underinsured persons took them on alternate days.

At ACRE, we worked with the Community Care Network (CCN), a nonprofit whose mission was to address health disparities. A mobile medical unit staffed by doctors and nurses visited our office in White Hall twice a month to provide medical care and prescription medicine to anyone in need. Without their efforts, many people would not have had medical care at all. Unfortunately, due to a reduction in funds, CCN could not maintain their service to our clients after the first five years. So the call from EJI was welcome.

ACRE was struggling to remain open. Most philanthropists and politicians didn't understand raw sewage in rural communities. An engineer friend from Georgia Tech told me the media was not interested in covering it because it was not sexy. A collaboration with EJI would be a lifeline for us.

I had an appointment to meet with Bryan Stevenson at the EJI office in Montgomery. The date of the meeting coincided with the date and the time I was to repeat a mammogram. My annual screening had shown some abnormalities and required additional testing. I had to decide whether to meet with this man I admired so much or to reschedule the meeting so that I wouldn't have to delay a much-needed medical procedure.

Through the years, my faith had grown stronger through adversity. I'd developed a ritual when I lived in North Carolina of opening my Bible to the 91st Psalm and reading it out loud in difficult times. One passage especially resonated with me:

Whoever dwells in the shelter of the Most High will rest in the shadow of the Almighty.

I will say of the Lord, "He is my refuge and my fortress, my God, in whom I trust."

It filled me with confidence that God was with me. This was one of those times I needed it. My mother liked to say that faith the size of a grain of mustard seed could move mountains. Because of my faith and belief that everything would be alright, I rescheduled the additional screening so I could meet Stevenson.

The day of the meeting, I nervously doodled on a writing pad while sitting in the small conference room in the EJI complex, trying to think of what I would say. When Bryan entered the room, I stood. He walked directly to me and extended his hand. Before I could say anything, he told me that he'd grown up in Delaware dealing with raw sewage. All I could think was, *Wow!* Here was a world-class attorney fighting for those who have been forgotten, who has dealt with the very problem I'd been fighting to alleviate. I realized we shared an understanding that most people lacked. My faith again had directed me to the place where I needed to be at that time.

Bryan told me that he wanted to support my work. I became a little overwhelmed, and tears fell from my eyes. I told him I had postponed my appointment to be rescreened for breast cancer because I thought this meeting was so important. He gave me a packet of information and offered me a job at EJI. I accepted.

Being at EJI allowed me to keep working on the wastewater problem in Lowndes County. I continued to receive calls from officials at the state health department about people with wastewater issues. One call was regarding a young woman, a teller at a local bank, who had obtained a mortgage on a home that was about eight years old. The home passed inspection as required by the bank. After she moved in with her children, the owners of the adjacent property complained that raw sewage from her home was spilling onto their pasture. To underscore the urgency, they said their cattle were walking through it.

I met health department officials at the home. It was a nice-looking house with a neatly kept lawn. It was hard to imagine anything was wrong with it. However, on closer inspection, there was no septic tank, just a pipe depositing sewage on the ground. When the homeowner purchased the home, she assumed the liability, although the lack of a septic tank had not been disclosed to her. I asked the health official, who was the department's regional environmentalist, how someone could sell a house to her and not tell her this.

He said it happened often and that there was no state law requiring this type of disclosure. I asked how the home had passed inspection. He replied, "All that is necessary is that the inspector flush the toilet. He flushed the toilet." There were other obvious questions: Had the previous owners been reported to the health department? Who had built the house, and who had sold the house to her? What was the relationship of the seller to the person who reported her? The homeowner was now facing arrest unless she paid for an expensive septic system that she could not afford. At least our involvement bought her more time.

Many more scenarios emerged. In one case, health officials asked me to go to the home of another resident who was being cited for not having a septic tank. I had been getting pressure from the health department, warning that they were going to begin arrests again, so I decided to invite a journalist, Bob Johnson from the Associated Press, to meet me there. The resident, named Shar, lived on a county road off Highway 80 on a five-acre plot of land owned by her mother. Her single-wide mobile home sat beyond her mother's home as we drove onto the property.

We entered Shar's home and sat in her living room. She told us she had one child who was autistic, and she was pregnant with a second child. She recounted how her family had to pay $800 for a perc test to keep her from being arrested. Now the health department was threatening again to have her arrested if she did not have a septic tank installed. The estimated cost was $10,000, and Shar's income averaged around $700 a month. There was no way she could pay for this. Threatening a young mother with arrest was not a solution.

I asked to see where the sewage was pooling. She took us outside and around to the back of her home, where sewage was flowing into a hole in the ground near the back door. Feces, toilet paper, and water were near the top of the hole. Although our visit was in October, the pit was teeming with mosquitoes, some sitting on the raw sewage. I was wearing a black dress that went just past my knees, black stockings, and heels. As I walked near the pit, I immediately felt bites on my legs and stepped back. My legs were covered with mosquito bites, and little drops of blood indicated that the mosquitoes had drawn blood.

The health department officials had told me they were going

to start arrests again because they were still waiting for us to receive the federal appropriation that had been approved nearly seven years earlier. I had done all I could do to try to get the EPA to release the funding, but to no avail. The thought of Shar's going to jail compelled me to get in touch with Senator Sessions's office. I told his aides about Shar and asked if they could intervene with the EPA. In a letter dated October 29, 2009, Sessions asked EPA administrator Lisa Jackson to look into it.

As all this was going on, I began to break out in a rash. The bumps were raised and mostly on the trunk of my body, with a few on my legs and one near my left ankle. I went to see Kim Hindi, a nurse practitioner, whom I'd worked with since my primary care doctor relocated. She was more than a medical provider and had listened to my stories about my work in Lowndes County. I asked her if I could have caught something from the mosquito bites, and she ordered blood tests.

The tests came back negative, but the rash remained. I asked Kim if I might have some illness that American doctors are not trained to treat. I had noticed that the climate was changing. We had more warm days. Mosquitoes were vectors of disease. I began to think about tropical diseases.

Kim referred me to a dermatologist, who thought it was a type of rosacea and prescribed creams to treat me. When they were not effective, he did a biopsy. The scar is still evident on the right side of my left foot just below my ankle. Still, he found no reason for the rash. After many weeks the rash went away, but my concern remained. I began to wear pants and long sleeves and boots to sites where I knew raw sewage was present. I also continued to wonder whether tropical diseases existed in our area.

Almost a year after Sen. Sessions sent his letter to Lisa Jackson, word came that we would be getting the grant from the EPA for a national demonstration project. We also discovered there were other national awardees for this program that had also been held up for eight years. The letter from Sen. Sessions helped move the process along not only for us, but also for other recipients of the appropriation. One official at the EPA told me that we were the only recipient that represented a poor community.

When we initially sought the appropriation, we thought we would be able to use the funds for septic tank installations for Lowndes County families. However, the EPA did not give us permission to do any construction projects. To end further delay, a supporter within the agency told us that we could only use it as a planning grant. So we revised our work plan, deciding instead to quantify the raw sewage problem.

Previously, we had focused our efforts on homes with no wastewater treatment at all because their occupants were targeted for arrest. No one had surveyed all households to determine the extent of the problem. Any effective long-term solution would involve finding out how many households were affected and whether they had septic tanks or were connected to municipal systems. We began to undertake an ambitious, long-needed fact-finding mission.

We divided the county's 714 square miles into five areas, roughly following the lines for county commission districts. A supporter within the local government gave us a copy of the county's 9-1-1 list. We also paid for copies of voter registration rolls that had addresses and sought additional information to prepare the most complete list possible of county residences. We set out to find trusted members of the community to conduct the survey, knowing we would have to break through residents' fear of prosecution and jail. Some of the communities were inhabited by compounds of relatives, and anyone not familiar with the area or known to the residents would not be welcomed.

We agreed that residents' identities would be concealed

so they could speak freely with us. We developed our survey forms based on a document from the Rural Communities Assistance Partnership, which is a national network of nonprofit organizations working to provide technical assistance, training, resources, and support to rural communities across the United States, tribal lands, and U.S. territories.

Surveyors fanned out across the county, and we met once a week to review findings. Our volunteers reported mostly positive experiences. When Black surveyors were apprehensive about how they would be received in white homes because of racism that was still prevalent, one volunteer shared her positive experience to alleviate any concerns. After she knocked on the door of the home, she was welcomed in. The resident called his neighbors and asked them to talk to her as well. Some experiences were not so favorable, but our venture was generally well received. Many people were happy we were finally collecting this information.

The survey revealed an array of wastewater issues affecting both homes and businesses across the county. Stunningly, they even occurred in townships that had wastewater treatment. We learned about residents who were paying wastewater fees but still had raw sewage backing up into their homes. Stories about sewage running into bathtubs and flooding houses were common. The problem was far greater than what the state health department was pursuing.

The biggest revelation for us was that the wastewater treatment technology that people were required to buy to avoid arrest was failing at high rates.

Thoughts about my mystery illness continued to bother me. Then one day I read a *New York Times* op-ed written by Dr. Peter Hotez, dean of the National School of Tropical Medicine and professor at Baylor College of Medicine in Houston.

It was titled "Tropical Disease: The New Plague of Poverty."
He wrote about diseases that are usually associated with
third-world countries, but which are increasingly found in the
United States, especially among poor people and minorities
and in the South, where the climate is warm. He called them
"the forgotten diseases of forgotten people." I read the op-ed
repeatedly. Using Google, I found contact information for him
and composed an email:

> I read your article in the New York Times and I am inter-
> ested in learning more. I am directing a project funded
> by the EPA that is examining the raw sewage issue in
> Lowndes County, Alabama. Many people in the area
> where I work are sick and there is an unusually high rate
> of asthma in the county. When I contacted the State De-
> partment of Public Health, they had no evidence of any
> diseases that could be caused by fecal contamination.
> They also have not recorded any tropical diseases. There
> must be some type of evidence because the raw sewage is
> so prevalent throughout the Black Belt region.
>
> Where is this data documented? How will doctors get
> information about what these diseases are? How does the
> public get this information? What are the diseases they
> should look for? What are the symptoms? We recently
> did a house-to-house survey and have documented the
> amount of raw sewage in this county, and we are pre-
> paring a master plan for addressing wastewater issues in
> poor rural communities. I would like to share it with you
> and get your comments as it relates to public health and
> tropical diseases.

In three hours I received an email response asking if I
would be in Atlanta the next week for the annual meeting

of the American Society for Tropical Medicine and Hygiene (ASTMH). It's the largest international scientific organization of experts dedicated to reducing the worldwide burden of tropical infectious diseases and improving global health. I hadn't planned to attend, but now I would.

I met Dr. Hotez and a small team of assistants in the lobby of the hotel hosting the event. He was pleasant to talk to as I described my experience with the rash and mosquito bites. He told me he wanted to send his parasitologist to Lowndes County to collect fecal samples to look for hookworm. I had only heard of hookworm a few times before and was nervous about the possibility that it existed in Lowndes County. During our conversation, I asked why he'd written the op-ed. He said it was because every time he mentioned neglected diseases of poverty in the United States, they were blamed on immigration. Then he said, "I was hoping a Catherine Flowers would reach out to me."

We began to prepare for the study. I informed the state environmentalist that we were going to do it. I also was talking constantly to Bryan Stevenson. He hired a nurse to take blood samples from participants, as we'd been directed to do. The needles were provided by a medical clinic affiliated with Partners in Health. We had regular conference calls with the people at Baylor and a few other partners in medicine. One conversation included Dr. Paul Farmer, a professor at Harvard Medical School and a co-founder of Partners in Health.

Dr. Rojelio Mejia drove to Alabama to collect the fecal samples from residents throughout Lowndes County. I even submitted a sample because of my exposure to raw sewage. The morning we began collecting samples, we drove to a compound where there were at least ten homes. We had to step over untreated sewage to get from home to home. Mejia, who told us to call him Rojelio, had to change from his dress shoes to boots because the sewage was everywhere. He tweeted a photo of the area and received responses from his colleagues around the world, who were surprised that the pictures were taken in the United States.

The residents initially eyed him with suspicion but wanted to participate in the study. They made it clear they did not trust the state health department and did not want them to have access to their samples. This was a hard call since the department was initially our partner in the study. However, we all agreed to maintain the participants' anonymity. After Rojelio visited several homes, I asked him to allow the community workers to return without him to collect samples. I knew they would be more comfortable with people they knew. Our volunteers were from the area and had longtime connections, sometimes blood relations, with the families.

Rojelio left Alabama with a few samples, and we had to wait for participants to let us know when the rest were ready to pick up. Once we finished gathering samples, we would take them to the National School of Tropical Medicine in Houston. Before leaving, Rojelio trained my team in how to store the samples and provided all the necessary supplies, including gloves. The registered nurse hired by EJI collected blood samples from some of the people providing fecal samples.

The day before I left for Houston, I went to EJI for a staff meeting. After the meeting ended, Bryan told me to get someone to go with me to Houston, rent a car to drive the samples there, and fly back. The next day I did as he instructed, and I delivered the samples, both blood and fecal, to Rojelio.

Once the testing was done, Rojelio called me with the news. He had found evidence of hookworm using DNA technology. Of fifty-five people tested, nineteen had hookworm. That's an alarming 34.5 percent.

This was momentous news, but we soon found that not

everyone was ready to accept it. The Alabama Health Department had initially been supportive, but when the hookworm results came back, they did an about-face. They denied the possibility of hookworm infections, issuing a public notice that said the peer-reviewed Baylor study did not find hookworm in Lowndes County. It was a stunning development. Clearly the state wasn't about to do anything to help the situation if the health department wouldn't admit it existed.

It's important to note that hookworm can not only be prevented with adequate sanitation, but also be treated. It's crucial that people know it exists, know its symptoms and their risks, and know they and their children can get help. It takes one to three days of anthelminthic medications—drugs that clear parasitic worms from the body. Nobody has to live with this debilitating parasite, and no one should suffer its effects needlessly. We know that it can cause diarrhea, fatigue, and anemia, and can impair cognitive and physical growth in children. How can any public official live with the knowledge that their inaction leaves people in jeopardy?

Fortunately, we had allies. Earthjustice, a nonprofit environmental justice law organization, helped us by filing a federal civil rights complaint against both the state and the Lowndes County health departments for failing to protect marginalized communities from the health consequences of inadequate sanitation and for spreading misinformation about risks that had been credibly identified. The complaint sought an independent investigation of discrimination in Alabama's prosecution of wastewater violations by Black people. It requested more study of failing septic systems and asked the department to educate the public about potential dangers to their health and how they could be treated for hookworm.

Despite the department's official position, some staffers within the department knew better. After all, Alabama had a long history with hookworm before it was thought to be eradicated. In fact, the establishment of the State Health Department Bureau of Sanitation came about as the result of hookworm infestation.

I received this note from a source in the health department showing that officials there hadn't always been in denial and historically had realized it was in the best interest of public health to provide wastewater solutions for all:

Here is a copy of the paper/presentation that we found a few months ago entitled "History of Sanitation" by O.G. Quenelle. I mentioned this paper to you at the first face-to-face meeting we had to discuss this project. Mr. Quenelle was, I think, one of my predecessors from the 1950s and 1960s. Back then, Environmental was called the Bureau of Sanitation . . .

For all of my career, I had been under the impression that our onsite (septic tank) program had originated to protect the public from various viruses and bacterial infections. While that was certainly a consideration, this paper flatly states that the findings of widespread hookworm infections was the real catalyst that led to the adoption of mandatory treatment of human wastes. The use of pit privies and septic tanks was strongly recommended in 1913 and, in 1927, the first legislation was passed that authorized the promulgation of regulations calling for their use.

It is interesting, regrettably, to note that the same public health malady that first triggered the requirements for mandatory treatment of human wastes has now reared its head as a potential threat today. After scores of years during which we assumed that the onsite program had eliminated this and other threats, we find that it is still among us. This study may prove to be an eye-opening experience.

The civil rights complaint was filed in September 2018 with the U.S. Department of Health and Human Services. As of February 2020, the department had not begun to investigate. We're still waiting.

Chapter 8

March 2015 marked the fiftieth anniversary of the march from Selma to Montgomery. It was a momentous occasion, with President Barack Obama and First Lady Michelle Obama among the thousands who walked across the Edmund Pettus Bridge. Veterans of the original march returned, including 103-year-old Amelia Boynton Robinson and Rep. John Lewis, both of whom were savagely beaten the first time they tried to cross the bridge. Even in a wheelchair, Mrs. Boynton was determined to cross that bridge again.

That week turned out to be a pivotal point in my life. Several events took place in Selma leading up to the emotional commemoration of Bloody Sunday, and I was invited to speak at one of them. The venue was the historic Brown Chapel AME Church, where the Selma to Montgomery march originated in 1965. It's now recognized as a sacred place for the voting rights movement. My speech was about how environmental injustice and poverty intersected in the raw sewage that flowed from forgotten people's homes.

Also speaking that day was Karenna Gore, a climate activist and daughter of former Vice President Al Gore. It was our first time meeting in person, but we had been exchanging emails. I remembered her from the dynamic speech she'd given at the 2000 Democratic Convention, where she nominated her father for president of the United States. Karenna first contacted me after reading about my work in an August 2014 article in *The New Republic* titled "The New Racism" by Jason Zengerle, who interviewed me in Lowndes County. He wrote:

> One recent afternoon, I met up with Catherine Flowers, who runs a Black Belt community organization called the Alabama Center for Rural Enterprise (ACRE). A few days earlier, over lunch at a Montgomery hot-dog shop, she told me, "My big issue is raw sewage." Now Flowers, a middle-aged African American woman who favors prim blue dresses and speaks in the patient tones of the elementary school teacher she once was, wanted to show me what she'd been talking about. We drove to the town of Fort Deposit in Lowndes County and pulled into a trailer park. Although we were less than a mile from town hall, Fort Deposit's municipal sewer line did not extend this far and, Flowers explained, the Lowndes soil had such a slow "percolation rate" that private septic systems were prohibitively expensive.
>
> "Watch where you step," Flowers said. She walked over to one of the mobile homes and pointed to a piece of PVC pipe jutting out from its base. "That's where they run the sewage out," she said, gesturing to a field in between houses that was covered with children's toys and human feces; bouncy balls and scraps of soiled toilet paper. Working with tropical disease experts at Baylor College of Medicine in Texas, ACRE had recently begun collecting fecal samples from residents of this trailer park

and others in the Black Belt for DNA testing. Of the 59 samples tested, 23 contained evidence of infection, primarily from hookworm. At one point, that parasite affected more than 40 percent of people in the South but was thought to have been eradicated in the United States in the early twentieth century.

Knowing we would both be in Selma, Karenna had reached out to me to discuss our mutual work, and I readily agreed. I knew that climate change was going to make the raw sewage problem worse, and it seemed like this could be an opportunity for us to bridge a gap and bring together people who cared about the environment with activists on the front lines of environmental justice. We met at the church moments before having to take our seats in the pulpit to wait our turns to speak.

The church was already full of people there for the program, or just to sit in such a legendary place, when a group arrived and sat in the first row. I immediately recognized Reverend Dr. William Barber, who stood out among the others. I greatly admired Barber's Moral Monday movement in North Carolina. He had mobilized a diverse coalition of activists to protest for causes such as health care access and voting rights, and had become a force to be reckoned with. I was delighted that he was there.

Barber has a huge presence, both in physical stature and in speaking style. His voice is a velvet baritone that he can lower to a mere whisper or raise to a resounding crescendo. A Duke University–trained theologian, he mixes scholarly and people-centered liberation theologies. Some compare him to Martin Luther King Jr. for his powerful oratory and ability to inspire a crowd. That day, he spoke about the principles of his moral movement, and how we should not get hung up on terms like "right" or "left" but instead choose right over wrong. I made a mental note to learn more about him because I had seldom heard a national leader frame the way forward with such clarity. I thought he might also be an ally in the campaign to bring equal access to sanitation to rural communities, and my instincts, once again, were right.

I also briefly met a reporter named Paul Lewis, who was the Washington correspondent for *The Guardian*. He was on his way to Uniontown, which was the face of environmental justice in Alabama at the time because coal ash was being dumped there from Tennessee. He and I talked about the possibility of *The Guardian*'s breaking the story about the parasite study once it was peer reviewed and published in a scholarly journal.

The people I connected with that week would change the trajectory of my life over the coming years. One of the most impactful was Karenna. She was preparing to launch the Center for Earth Ethics (CCE) at Union Theological Seminary, where she had earned her master's degree in divinity. She asked me to be a part of it.

After our time in Selma, I visited with her in New York and discussed her vision for the center. It would study the climate crisis through a moral lens, searching for solutions to environmental injustice in the context of history, culture, and spiritual beliefs. It would honor indigenous wisdom, an approach that appealed to me. Karenna and I found we had mutual respect for the knowledge of indigenous peoples. I'd studied Native American history while pursuing my master's degree at the University of Nebraska at Kearney, and Karenna considered native voices essential to her mission. We also found we shared an appreciation for Vine Deloria, a Native American author and historian.

I attended the commencement services for Union Theological Seminary, which took place the same day as the launch of the Center for Earth Ethics. Union is in Morningside Heights, New York City, across from Columbia University and down the street from Barnard College. For years, I had toyed with the possibility of attending seminary, and Union would have been my first choice. It's nondenominational and committed to training people of all faiths who are called to the work of social justice. Many respected theologians who helped shape liberal Christian theology have studied and taught there.

Commencement services were held in the courtyard of the seminary building, a brick and limestone English Gothic revival structure completed in 1910 and listed on the National Historic Register. It was a beautiful sunny day as I sat waiting for the service to start. Then came the procession, marching to the beat of drums, waving rainbow flags, and led by Dr. Cornel West. A choir of Union students sang a mean version of a gospel song, and it was time for the speakers. One of them was Karenna's father, former Vice President Al Gore.

Afterward, there was a dinner for supporters of the Center for Earth Ethics. In the room were notables, including former Senator Bill Bradley, who had been Gore's running mate in 2000, and Judith and Bill Moyers. I was seated at the table with Reverend Dr. Liz Theoharis from Kairos, The Center for Religions, Rights, and Social Justice, an organization committed to uniting the poor as a force in a broad, transformative movement to end poverty. She would later become co-chair of the New Poor People's Campaign with Rev. Barber. I looked around in awe. How did I ever get here? I wondered.

Karenna came over during dinner and asked if I could make a three-minute speech. I'm usually calm about public speaking, but this time I was very nervous because of who was in the audience. There wasn't time to organize a speech, so I decided just to speak from my heart. I was in impressive company. Karenna had also asked Lyla June Johnston and Jarid

Manos to speak. Lyla, a poet and musician, has been described as an "indigenous eco-Tubman." Jarid is the author of the book *Ghetto Plainsman* and founder of the Great Plains Restoration Council.

I practically held my breath until it was time to speak. When Karenna introduced me, I walked to the front of the room. I said that I was a country girl from Lowndes County, Alabama. I told about the sewage problem and how climate change would make it worse. I explained that the tropical parasites discovered in Lowndes County were an urgent warning. I ended by saying rural people are in touch with the natural world and recognize the changes occurring around us. Our wisdom must be included in the search for solutions.

When I finished, the audience members were on their feet, to my amazement. It was a powerful moment. But by the time I returned to my seat, my mind was already working on my next move. How was I going to get Al Gore to take a picture with me? It turned out I didn't even have to ask. He came to me and praised my speech, and a member of his party offered to take a picture. I was honored and overjoyed to have captured a memory of that night, thanks to Karenna.

Much of my role at CEE involved speaking to influencers in New York about rural biases and inequality. It helped me to establish the connection between infrastructure and health inequities and climate change. But that summer, representing CEE, I went to Appalachia to join a group led by John Wessel-McCoy from Kairos. Kairos was working to build a New Poor People's Campaign, and this trip was part of that effort. Along the way, I met other rural environmental justice activists who had experience with inadequate wastewater infrastructure.

Our trip began in West Virginia. After breakfast, we visited the former Whipple Company Store, an old company store that is now a museum. Labor historian Wess Harris told the wretched history of the sexual exploitation of women in the mining town by company men. When their husbands or sons were injured in the mines and therefore not earning pay, women could receive what was called "Esau scrip," a type of loan that they could use to buy food or other necessities. The name Esau comes from the book of Genesis, and the story of Esau, who sold his birthright to his younger brother Jacob in exchange for food. Sadly, one of the paradoxes of religion is it is sometimes used to sanction or underscore inequality and exploitation.

The women didn't have jobs of their own, so they had no money to repay the scrip. If their men didn't return to work and start making money again, the women had to sexually submit to the men running the coal company. A third-floor room in the store was called the "rape room." The place was haunting, and the story was eerily like some I'd heard about plantations and sharecropping, yet this was a mining town.

In one of the rooms in the store, I was surprised to see a picture of Black people from the town, which I had thought was all white. It helped me to understand the kinship between rural folk who simply want to take care of their families, whether they are Black or white.

As we traveled through West Virginia, Kentucky, and Tennessee, I continued to see commonalities with the Black Belt. I realized Appalachia was like Lowndes County, except that most people I met were white. Both had long histories of exploiting people's labor and pillaging women. In Appalachia, where the tops of mountains were blown off to mine coal, it appeared the exploitation also extended to nature.

As we traveled, I asked about wastewater problems and learned in each rural community we visited that it was not uncommon to see raw sewage on the ground. Another common thread was that the communities that we visited were all very religious. Many of our meetings were with pastors or at churches, and we had prayer and reflection nightly.

After that trip, I continued hearing about sewage issues outside of Lowndes County. People from other parts of Alabama were calling me. I met with a group of ministers in a Black Belt county who talked about sanitation problems at their rural churches. A student at Duke University told me about the septic system his family had purchased in Marengo County, Alabama, that had begun to fail just a few months after it was installed and approved by health officials. An attorney from a middle-class white family in Alabama said her parents were embarrassed to have visitors at their home at times because of the overpowering smell of raw sewage, even though they were connected to a municipal wastewater system. Cherri Foytlin, a Gulf Coast activist who'd been in my group touring Appalachia, told me about St. James Parish in southeastern Louisiana, where people were having wastewater problems.

As word got out about our hookworm study, I received invitations to speak from around the United States, but I could not discuss the findings in detail until the peer-review process was completed. When people heard about Americans living among untreated waste, they were horrified and wanted to hear more. At the same time, climate change was finally a "hot topic," and the intersection between climate change and the waste problem was becoming more apparent. Yet the sewage issue was still not covered much by the national media. I thought back to when my engineer friend had told me the media would not cover it because it wasn't sexy enough.

The venues where I went to listen or to speak were getting bigger and farther from home. Then in December 2015, I had the opportunity to go to the biggest one of all: the United Nations Climate Change Conference in Paris. This was where the Paris Agreement—a global commitment to reduce greenhouse gas emissions—was negotiated. Representatives from the European Union and 195 nations attended. I would represent the Center for Earth Ethics as an observer of the climate treaty negotiations.

I'd never been to Europe, and it was exciting. The food on the Air France flight from Atlanta to Paris was wonderful. It made me look forward to eating the delicacies for which Paris was known. I also looked forward to possibly visiting the Louvre, Notre-Dame Cathedral, and the Eiffel Tower. A terrible terrorist attack had occurred just days before, but I had no fear. I was going to engage with people from around the world to learn about climate change and its impacts. It was an awesome feeling, and a little bit surreal.

I arrived at the airport in Paris and took a taxi to a side event in a school in a small town outside the city. There, I met with students and teachers from HBCUs around the United States. The NAACP had a presence too. I was happy to see Jacqui Patterson, director of the NAACP Climate Justice Program, who had once visited Lowndes County. After I spoke, a number of young people came to me to say they, too, had seen raw sewage in their communities. This was becoming a pattern. Something most people didn't talk about turned out to be something many had seen or experienced. I spoke at several more side events during the two weeks of the conference, and my story was well received.

Back in the United States, I spoke at the Health and Climate Symposium at the Carter Center in Atlanta, receiving a standing ovation after discussing the nitty-gritty of rural people's living on the front lines of climate change with raw sewage on the ground.

Momentum was growing. Maybe raw sewage was sexy after all.

I was in DC on business in December 2016 when I received a call from Senator Cory Booker of New Jersey. His staff had let me know to expect it, but when I heard him on the other end of the phone, I was still a little stunned. He told me he wanted to be "the environmental justice senator." It was my first and only time hearing that from a senator. He asked about the parasite study and how the idea to do it had come about. I told him the whole story, starting with the mosquito bites. He was interested in finding a way to address neglected diseases of poverty, and he told me he wanted to come to Lowndes County.

Six months later, he arrived in Montgomery. We planned to meet for dinner the night before I took him to Lowndes County. He is a vegan, so I arranged for us to eat at Central, a restaurant that offered a few vegetarian options and that was conveniently located next door to EJI. Standing near the door, I waited with my brother for him to arrive. Soon Bryan Stevenson joined us, and then Booker walked in, looking very unassuming in his jeans. This was a first meeting for all of us, but we knew each other's work. Being at the table with one of the best social justice attorneys in the world and a Rhodes scholar who aspired to be the leading environmental justice senator was like being in social justice heaven. When we were joined by Mustafa Santiago Ali, vice president for environmental justice at the National Wildlife Federation, it got even more heavenly.

The next day, it was time to come back down to Earth in Lowndes County. Our first stop was at a single-wide mobile home where a disabled veteran lived near the Lowndes Interpretive Center off of Highway 80. A short walk from the civil rights trail, the veteran's backyard held a pit full of waste piped straight from his toilet.

I had been riding in the car with Booker and two aides. Before getting out of the car, I rubbed Skin So Soft on my arms to fend off mosquitoes. My sinuses flare up when I use insecticides, and Avon's Skin So Soft Bath Oil usually does the job. This time it didn't. When I stepped outside, I was immediately attacked by mosquitoes, and soon my arms were covered with bites. As if on cue, the bugs reenacted the scene that had started the hookworm study. Booker remarked on how the bugs seemed to be drawn to me.

As we walked to the back of the house, other people joined us, including a crew from *National Geographic*. We reached the pit, and Booker stared in disbelief. I had once filmed the pit because it was often full of both sewage and life. Mosquitoes were visible, and so were the bulging eyes of frogs semi-emerged in the human effluent.

The next home we visited had a failing septic system. The homeowner had disconnected it after sewage backed up into her bathtub. It was now flowing into a wooded area behind her house. Again, the mosquitoes descended. This time, a *National Geographic* producer sprayed Booker's clothes with a repellant that she said they used when filming in tropical areas. Yet we weren't in a developing nation. We were in Lowndes County, near the Alabama state capital.

The home was on the family's land along the Selma to Montgomery march trail. The owner's grandmother had housed marchers there. The owner's mother had been a plaintiff in a major civil rights case that challenged the exclusion of women from jury service. And the owner herself was one of the volunteers who had conducted our house-to-house survey to document problems with sewage.

The final home we visited was in the town of Hayneville. There, I witnessed a conversation that struck me as miraculous between Booker and the homeowners' daughter. I had been visiting this home for years, sometimes with visitors and sometimes alone. Each time I went there, I talked to the owner, Ms. Charlie Mae, or her husband. Her adult daughter, Steviana, would be present but rarely reacted beyond nodding her head or saying hello.

Steviana was sitting outside when we approached the house. Booker walked over to her, knelt beside her chair, introduced himself, and told her he was there to learn about the wastewater problem. For the first time, I saw Steviana perk up. She began describing the problem. I realized Booker had a distinct way with people, creating comfort and trust. He seemed deeply interested in what they had to say, and Steviana responded to that authentic concern.

She told how her family had struggled with sewage backing into their home for years, even though they paid a fee for municipal service. Steviana left Alabama for a time, only to return to the same problem. Sewage flowed not only into their neatly kept brick home, but also into their otherwise tidy front yard. Their street, lined with homes, is near the town's sewage lagoon. Instead of reliable wastewater treatment, residents of the neighborhood get a different kind of service from the town: when they call to complain about sewage in their homes or yards, sometimes several times in a week, the city sends workers in a truck to pump it out of their yard. Steviana's family had replaced their flooring numerous times.

Suddenly, Steviana asked everyone to be quiet and listen. She is blind and has a keen sense of hearing. "Do you hear that gurgling sound?" she asked. "Whenever we hear that gurgling sound, it is an indication that the toilet will overflow." A few days later, their home again was flooded with raw sewage. This time her family had to take out a loan to replace the flooring.

We were getting closer to the publication of our parasite study. Back in 2015, I had told Paul Lewis of *The Guardian* that his publication could break the story when the time came. I kept my promise and let him know. It turned out that Ed Pilkington, chief reporter for *The Guardian*, would be writing the story. Ed is British, with a history degree from Queens College at Cambridge, and unlike many reporters who visit the area, he came with a refreshing historical perspective. He knew the history of the South, and he also made comparisons to what he had seen in India.

Ed was shocked to see raw sewage on the ground. It is always amazing to me to hear people voice dismay about something that I have known for many, many years. It reminds me that this is, indeed, America's dirty secret. We have to unveil that secret if we are to find sustainable solutions.

The study went live September 17, 2017, in the *American Journal of Tropical Medicine and Hygiene*. It drew international attention, not only because it was important medical news, but also because it revealed a little-known side of the United States, although in clinical terms. It remains the most downloaded article from that journal.

Now *The Guardian* was free to publish its story. Ed took a narrative approach, painting a stark picture of the raw sewage problem, the diseases associated with exposure, and the gaping chasm between rich and poor in the United States. The headline proclaimed that "in America, the world's richest country, hookworm, a parasitic disease found in areas of extreme poverty, is rampant, the first study of its kind in modern times shows."

The story ran internationally and provided a view of rural America that was unknown to most of the world and, strangely, even to most of the United States.

"Scientists in Houston, Texas, have lifted the lid on one of America's darkest and deepest secrets: that hidden beneath fabulous wealth, the U.S. tolerates poverty-related illness at levels comparable to the world's poorest countries," Ed wrote. "More than one in three people sampled in a poor area of Alabama tested positive for traces of hookworm, a gastrointestinal parasite that was thought to have been eradicated from the US decades ago. The long-awaited findings, revealed by *The Guardian* for the first time, are a wake-up call for the world's only superpower as it grapples with growing inequality."

Most of the news coverage that followed focused on hookworm, but other parasites were detected as well. Stool samples were collected for fifty-five individuals. Of these, nineteen (34.5 percent) were positive for hookworm, four (7.3 percent) for roundworm, *Strongyloides stercoralis*, and one (1.8 percent) for *Entamoeba histolytica*, a parasite that can cause severe diarrhea. Finally, the dirty truth about sewage and inequality in rural America was official.

It was about to become even more public.

On a brisk December morning in 2017, I became tour guide for a very special group. This time, our guest represented the United Nations, and with him came a media entourage to capture the story. It was a chance to take our fight to a new level.

I had worked with JoAnn Kamuf Ward and Inga Winkler of Columbia University on framing the sewage problem in human-rights terms. JoAnn is director of the Human Rights in the U.S. Project of the Human Rights Institute at Columbia Law School, and also supervises the Human Rights Clinic. She focuses on inequality and social injustice within U.S. borders. I met her through my affiliation with the National Coalition for the Human Right to Water and Sanitation. We have collaborated on research and co-authored briefings about the waste problem in rural America, as well as partnered on international and domestic advocacy to improve access to basic services.

The first thing I noticed about Inga Winkler was her German accent. She is a lecturer at the Institute for the Study of Human Rights at Columbia University and the director of undergraduate studies for the human-rights program. Before joining Columbia, Inga was legal advisor to Catarina de Albuquerque, the United Nations' special rapporteur on human rights to water and sanitation.

I met Inga when I presented testimony to de Albuquerque during an official visit to the United States. Now Dr. Philip Alston was a UN Special Rapporteur and had been invited by President Obama to visit sites in the United States. When we learned he was coming, JoAnn and Inga helped me prepare a letter inviting Alston to Lowndes County. We set out to entice him with a compelling argument that the raw sewage issue was also a poverty issue. Our approach to addressing waste had not been taken in the United States before. This would be an opportunity to take the issue to the United Nations Human Rights Council and the world.

The letter succeeded as we had hoped. We were excited to learn Alston would come to Alabama, and as part of the trip, he would tour Lowndes County, accompanied by members of the international, national, and local press. Now we had to start planning logistics. We chose two locations to visit and decided to limit the number of vehicles traveling the back roads to minimize disruption.

Because the threat of arrests for raw sewage still loomed,

I requested that the press not reveal the identities of the people we visited or their locations in the county unless the people themselves gave permission. No areas were to be photographed without the permission of the homeowners. Experience has taught me that the way to garner trust is to respect the wishes of people who put their freedom on the line in pursuit of solutions. Also, I wanted people to speak freely without fear of retribution.

This would be an important opportunity for Alston, his entourage, and the media. It's vital for those who can influence policy to be proximate to the situation—to see things in person, as they are. One obstacle to finding sustainable solutions to rural problems is that policymakers and other influential people usually lack experience in the sorts of communities that need their help. Helicoptering into a town hall meeting or to talk to local officials does not adequately convey the gravity of human suffering.

That's why it is crucial to have local guides with credibility and trust in their communities. The homes where we take guests are places that you will not find using Google maps or your GPS. We go to places that have been out of sight and out of mind for years. Dr. Alston's visit would provide him and others with a rare perspective that few receive.

The day of the visit, the weather was unusually cold, and a rare snowfall was expected. I am sure it seemed like we were traveling forever as we left the interstate highway, drove through a small town, and crossed railroad tracks to reach a family compound of mobile homes. The patriarch of the family, a preacher, was waiting for us. Disregarding our instructions, one of the press crew approached the gentleman with his camera. The homeowner began to walk away out of fear of reprisals. Alston, in his stern Australian accent, told the crew to cut off all cameras.

This moment of empathy and understanding gave me profound respect for Alston. Photographs of the streams of waste around the trailers could have propelled the story into greater circulation internationally. Yet Alston was more concerned about hearing from the preacher, whom I'll call Mr. B.

Alston told Mr. B that he was there to learn from him. Relaxing a little, Mr. B began to talk. He told Alston about the exorbitant cost of an onsite system that his family could not afford. Then he led him through the property, showing where sewage flowed. We stopped at one of the trailers and saw a pit of effluent outside the home and more waste underneath it. The entourage stood quietly in apparent horror, their breath steamy in the frosty morning.

The next location was another cluster of mobile homes. This visit was led by Aaron Thigpen, one of ACRE's community organizers. Aaron was a relative of the homeowners and had lived in Fort Deposit for all of his twenty-nine years. The homeowners chose him to speak on their behalf. He showed Alston around the site, where five members of his extended family, including two minor children and an eighteen-year-old with Down syndrome, live.

I had been here with Aaron many times before. Their house discharged its waste through straight pipes that released the effluent into fetid open-air pools. As in many other rural sites, their sewage ran into wooded areas or across grassy fields. In this case, water lines ran along the area where the waste collected.

A reporter asked Alston if he had seen this before.

His response: "I have not seen this in the first world."

Chapter 9

On a beautiful sunny day in early 2018, I took another very special group to tour Lowndes County. Reverend William Barber, the voice of the New Poor People's Campaign, was finally here. I was serving on the national steering committee for the campaign, and I admired his leadership, his powerful presence, and his message of uniting diverse people for the common good.

I'd been wanting to show him the atrocious living conditions of poor people in Lowndes County for some time, and his visit was a milestone for me. The timing was excellent. I'd seen him speak in Selma two years earlier. Now it was almost time for another annual commemoration of the march to Montgomery, and he would be a prominent speaker, this time with Lowndes County on his mind.

Rev. Barber was accompanied by Reverend Liz Theoharis, who led a group of men and women from the Repairers of the Breach, Kairos Center, at Union Theological Seminary. A small group of journalists joined us, along with Dara Kell, an award-winning documentary filmmaker and a native of South Africa. In November 2016 she had accompanied me in

Standing Rock, where I went to stand in solidarity with my indigenous sisters and brothers to protest a pipeline that could contaminate their water source. It was another example of rural America's being neglected and exploited without regard for the people living there.

Dara had documented my experience there, and I knew that I could count on her in Lowndes County to respect the families and be mindful of protecting their privacy if they requested it. John Wessel-McCoy, who had led the trip through Appalachia, was with us too. A grassroots organizer and guitar-playing folk singer, he was also a graduate of Union Theological Seminary.

This day was different than other times I'd given tours because of our guests' belief in the social justice teachings of the Gospels. In my mind, I imagined they were disciples from the Bible. Unlike other prominent people who simply passed through on their way to Selma, they came to hear and see people who had been rendered voiceless because of poverty and inequality.

Just like when the U.N. special rapporteur visited, we stopped first in the town of Fort Deposit. It's the largest town in Lowndes County, originally built as a fort to supply Andrew Jackson and his troops during the war with the Creeks, who were indigenous to the area. The town was incorporated in 1891.

Like many places in the South, Fort Deposit has a history of oppression of its Black population. One incident was especially horrific. On August 14, 1965, SNCC leader Stokely Carmichael led a group of local youth in a protest there against segregated businesses. He was joined by Jonathan Daniels, a white Episcopal seminarian, four SNCC workers, and a white Catholic priest, Reverend Richard Morrisroe. They were all arrested and taken to jail in Hayneville, the county seat.

The day they were released, Jonathan Daniels went with

Father Morrisroe and one of the teens, Ruby Sales, to a store to buy food. Before they even entered the store, Tom Coleman, a sheriff's department volunteer, opened fire, shooting Daniels straight on and Morrisroe in the back. Daniels was killed instantly, and Morrisroe was seriously wounded.

Coleman called the state's public safety director from the sheriff's office and told him he had just shot two preachers. He was arrested, maybe due to widespread media coverage, but his trial—for manslaughter—was a sham. The all-white, all-male jury deliberated less than two hours and acquitted him. Jurors stepped from the jury box to shake his hand. One was heard to tell him he'd see him duck hunting the next Saturday.

Coleman was the son of longtime sheriff Jesse Coleman and the brother of Hulda Coleman, the woman who'd served as school superintendent while I was in high school. One of my first actions as a student activist had been encouraging an investigation that led to her resignation.

This history was not lost on me as I set out with the group of ministers. In Fort Deposit, we gathered at the town hall. The day was so meaningful to me that I remember even the smallest details vividly.

Rev. Barber is pastor of the Greenleaf Christian Church in Goldsboro, North Carolina, and a bishop for the Disciples of Christ, a Protestant denomination. Tall and broad, he was a striking figure that day in black dress pants, a black button-down vest, and a purple shirt with a white preacher's collar and white cuffs fastened by cuff links. Rev. Theoharis dressed conservatively in a black skirt, black tights, a white clerical collar, and a turquoise blouse. I wore my usual black slacks, a black jacket, and boots, deviating slightly from my normal uniform with an animal-print top. We held a brief press conference for the media, and Rev. Barber explained why he was in Lowndes County.

Afterward, I began our orientation for visitors while still standing in the parking lot. We were going to visit the homes of families who were subject to arrest; therefore, journalists needed to ask permission to film or photograph them or their homes and refrain from using details that could identify them.

To help explain the injustice of what they were about to see, I told the group about a situation that seemed to me a perfect example of how inequality plays out in poor rural communities. Businesses at the I-65 exchange were having problems with sewage. It was so bad that the owners of a service station there had to have their septic tanks pumped at least once a week, a town employee had told Duke University faculty and students when they visited the area. But instead of facing prosecution for their septic problems, they benefitted from a federal grant to extend the municipal wastewater system to them. In contrast, people living less than half a mile from the town hall lived with raw sewage on the ground. Relief was allotted based on privilege, not public health.

A dirt road took us to the first group of homes on our tour, a site that Dr. Alston had also visited. Several rusty single-wide trailers stood on the property. Other small homes and a few churches were nearby. A train whistled in the distance. This was a deeply religious community, I thought to myself, but the rewards promised by the prosperity gospel clearly had clearly not arrived.

Rev. Barber was welcomed by all who saw him. We walked around the homes in the compound, observing streams of sewage in the yard. Effluent leaked from underneath one mobile home, while a pipe discharged waste into a small pit. At another home, sewage flowed through a patch of very green grass. Toilet paper and feces lay on the ground.

In the compassionate tones of someone accustomed to ministering to the broken, Rev. Barber spoke with the family patriarch, who said he was a Pentecostal pastor. Rev. Barber asked him to lead us in prayer. Those of us who were "churched" understood that as a sign of deep respect. We all touched one another in silence as he prayed aloud. This was an uncommon day. Rev. Barber had brought his moral crusade to the backwoods of Lowndes County.

After hearing the struggles of this impoverished family, we set out for our next destination. I had asked everyone to write down the directions because I knew there would be places along the route where their GPS would not work, nor would they have phone service. Journalists from Canada occupied one of the cars in the entourage. On the phone before our meeting, I had told one of them to stay with us in the caravan or to write down the directions. She had laughed and said she had traveled all over the world. I thought to myself, she has not been in rural Lowndes County.

Sometimes even writing down the directions to our locations would not preclude people from getting lost if they were new to a rural area, and this was the case going to the next home, when that same journalist from Canada found her world travels hadn't prepared her for our roads.

My car was the lead vehicle, driven by my brother, who knew his way around better than I did. A baseball player and a preacher, he'd played in dirt fields and preached in churches throughout the county. We were headed to an unpaved road deep in the interior of the county, and I was counting on him.

It took about a half hour to make the trip from Fort Deposit. The last landmark we passed was a church. After that, the dirt road proceeded through deep woods. Today it's the Collirene

Cutoff Road, but it used to be called "The Nigger Foot Road," a remnant of the racial terror that was once a way of life here. Clouds of red dust enveloped the vehicles. Cresting a hill, we turned right at a brown, single-wide mobile home. Behind it was the blue trailer where Pamela Rush lived with her two children.

I walked to the door of her home and knocked. The steps to her front door were in serious disrepair, so I asked everyone to stay outside unless she invited them in. Pamela came out and greeted us, neatly dressed in a yellow blouse and black slacks.

I introduced her to our special guests, and Rev. Barber greeted her warmly. I listened once again as Pam described her personal story of being trapped in poverty, and watched as others heard it for the first time. Pam spoke timidly. "I am poor, and I don't have much," she said. "I am trying to take care of my two children." Rev. Barber listened attentively, his left hand on his cane and his right hand in his pocket, while Pam spoke. She lacked possessions and money, but she possessed the courage to show the world what life was like for a low-income family in rural America.

She led us to the rear of the trailer so we could see where the sewage was straight-piped onto her backyard. It remained on the ground near her back door. A child's guitar lay close by. Pam described living in fear of being arrested. There was no way she could afford a septic system on her income. The high water table in the area required a specially engineered system. Just getting the perc test and design done was way out of her reach.

Pam's family members had already been punished for their poverty. One of her sisters had been arrested several years earlier for not having a septic tank. Later, another sister was arrested and fined when she couldn't pay a garbage bill. When asked why she dared tell her story, Pam said she trusted me and hoped help would come, not only for her family, but also for others in the same situation.

Pam led us back to her front door. One step was missing and the others were unsteady as we followed her inside. From the small living room, she turned right into a bedroom where mold covered the walls. Visitors looked in disbelief. We saw the kitchen, where the refrigerator doors had rusted in the damp air and cheaply made cabinets were collapsing.

Then we walked into the bedroom, where Pam shared a queen-size bed with her young daughter. Hanging from the headboard was the mask for the CPAP machine that helped the child breathe at night, a challenge complicated by asthma and mold. It was a chilling sight. *No child should need this kind of equipment just to breathe*, I thought. Back in the living room, a small gas heater hung on the wall. Pam said her family slept near the heater on cold nights to keep warm.

Pam shared a copy of her mortgage. Her brother purchased the home in the mid-1990s for $113,000, and she still owed close to $13,000. There was no equity in the home. It had started losing value as soon as it was pulled off the lot. Pam was trapped. Here was an example of how economic structures perpetuate inequality, stacking the odds against escaping poverty.

Although I had heard Pam's story before, I was overwhelmed with emotion. I thanked the Reverends Barber and Theoharis for coming to see this firsthand. Rev. Barber promised he would bring others and tell the world what he saw. He walked down the steps and into the yard, and then stood outside alone for what seemed like a long time. We did not approach him, but rather let him reflect. I suspected he was flooded with emotion too.

Several weeks later, Pam was testifying before Congress

as part of the New Poor People's Campaign. Rev. Barber had quickly made good on his word.

Since the publication of the parasite study, I'd begun receiving more invitations to events related to science, which had been one of my favorite subjects in school. Secretly, I had wanted to become an astronaut, but during my youth there were not many women astronauts. Now I felt like an explorer in the world of parasitology.

Since 2014 I had been working with graduate students from Duke University, bringing them to Lowndes County to learn about wastewater issues. I also taught them to shed their assumptions about local people and instead to listen to their wisdom and insights. One of the students was Ryan Justus. He had attended and worked at Wheaton College, in Wheaton, Illinois, and at his suggestion the college had invited me to be a keynote speaker for the Wheaton Science Symposium. I immediately accepted, although this was my first time hearing about Wheaton. I did some research and learned it was a prestigious liberal arts college and graduate school founded by evangelicals. It was one of many stops along the Underground Railroad and was deeply involved in the abolitionist movement.

Throughout this journey, I have always acknowledged that I am a person of faith, but one very tolerant of others and their religious traditions. My approach to religion and spirituality is to celebrate the traditions we all commonly share. I look for the commonality in every situation, a lesson I learned while working with Bob Woodson. If we can find common ground, we're more likely to find solutions together.

I decided to talk at the symposium about rural inequality. The night of my speech, I noticed the auditorium quickly filling with people. I had carefully prepared my address because this was a different type of audience for me. Before leaving for Wheaton, some of my friends had expressed concern about whether I would be accepted in a conservative Christian environment. They thought I might encounter resistance to my message.

I did not feel that way. From the time I arrived on campus, I felt very comfortable. On the day of my keynote address, I visited three science classes and a chapel service. The speaker at the chapel service talked about climate change. In the classrooms, students and teachers prayed. This was not awkward for me, because I always silently pray before a test or before I speak to an audience. Before this trip, I had asked God to let His will be done.

That evening, I approached the podium after playing a brief video about the wastewater situation in Alabama. I knew the audience was stunned before I even started. I looked at the faces sitting in front of me. Most were young, and many had probably gone on mission trips where they'd encountered poor sanitation. Many were shocked that these conditions existed in the United States.

I said my usual silent prayer and looked at my prepared text and opened my mouth to speak. But something unusual came over me. Instead of reading from my speech, I said, "I am going to do something I usually do not do. I will put aside my prepared speech and instead speak to you from my Christian experience."

My speech was titled "America's Dirty Secret: Poverty and Parasites." The words flowed as I spoke about my youth in rural Lowndes County and my Christian experience. I talked about how faith propelled us to work for justice and requested us to be merciful to all. I spoke about civil rights and environmental justice. I told them about my thirst for righteousness, which sometimes called me to exercise my faith by walking to churches with outdoor toilets the first and third Sundays, or to hear sermons preached by circuit pastors on the second and fourth Sundays. I said our faith should compel us to work to overcome inequality in America, especially in rural communities. It was our Christian duty.

I spoke for approximately forty minutes. When I ended, I was pleasantly surprised to receive a standing ovation. A question-and-answer session followed, and after it was over, people waited in a long line to talk to me. One student said generations of his family were dairy farmers in rural Wisconsin and he had seen firsthand the wastewater problems I described. He thanked me for bringing rural life to the forefront and hoped that rural communities and rural culture no longer would be neglected by public policy. The student editor of the school's newspaper, *The Wheaton Record*, asked to interview me before I left. She thought more students should hear what I had to say. The interview appeared under a title that felt just right to me: *Faith Activism*.

While our work was gaining attention in the scientific and faith communities, it also caught the interest of politicians, including members of Congress. In March 2018, Senator Bernie Sanders of Vermont invited me to take part in a town hall meeting in Washington, DC, titled "Inequality in America," along with documentary filmmaker Michael Moore, Senator Elizabeth Warren, and Darrick Hamilton, professor of economics and urban policy at The New School. After introductions and pictures, we walked to the Capitol Visitor Center, where long lines were forming.

The town hall was live-streamed, and more than two million viewers eventually watched it. Sanders began by asking me to describe what I saw every day. I painted a verbal picture of the wastewater situation in Lowndes County and framed it with a historical perspective.

"Well, I work primarily in rural communities," I began. "I grew up in Alabama's Black Belt. It is one of the poorest areas in the United States, and the area is populated primarily by people of color. At one point at the end of the international slave trade, Montgomery was the center of the domestic slave trade. A lot of people that are in the Black Belt can trace their heritage back to those days. I think that the structural poverty, and the political structures that are in place, reinforce the kind of poverty that exists in the area today.

"Since I've returned to the area . . . I've seen raw sewage underneath mobile homes. I have seen people invest in on-site septic systems that they are told by the State Health Department to purchase, and sewage is running back into their homes. . . . That is just an atrocity, that at this particular time in our history, when we have the wealthiest people in the world in the wealthiest nation in the world, that we allow this kind of thing here in the United States of America."

Sen. Warren chimed in, framing the problem differently. "Okay, so I want to pick up on her point because I've read your work, and you're really doing amazing work and trying to bring attention to this, but there's this Catch-22 right in the middle of it," she said. "That you talk about how there's basically no sewage infrastructure, think about that, in places where people live in America, and as you point out, because of the way the land is, it's not like you can just dig a septic and you'll be okay, you just literally can't do that.

"This is why sewage backs up into people's houses, into their trailers; but business won't come to this area, because there's no sewage infrastructure. And if there's no business, there's no tax space to build any sewage infrastructure. Do you see a pattern here of how this works? So you get these areas of poverty that just get locked in poverty, you see this some on Native American reservations. Areas where, right now, a third of all people who are living on tribal lands have no access to the internet. None. Zero.

"Who can run a business in the twenty-first century without it, who can run a library without access to the internet? And so without it, nobody comes, nobody makes the investment, and if nobody comes and nobody makes the investments, then you create these circles of poverty that just wipe out opportunity for anyone. And this goes back to this fundamental question. This is where our federal government should be making investments. Investments in making opportunity."

I listened intently as she spoke. I thought she was an ally. But clearly she did not understand her analysis was flawed. The notion that investing in the business community would take care of the long-term negligence of poor and rural communities was a failed paradigm. She was partly right, but she was missing the bigger point. Yes, the Catch-22 Warren described exists. Businesses won't come where there's no infrastructure, and that just perpetuates inequality in Lowndes County and other rural places.

But there's a deeper, more fundamental issue than how businesses make decisions. It goes to why there's no infrastructure in the first place. It's about how these areas have historically been overlooked because of who lives there. It's about who is and has been considered worthy—by politicians, bureaucrats, even society at large. And even though rural bias is real, rural communities aren't the only places where infrastructure is lacking. Just look at Flint, Michigan.

As Michael Moore explained: "The water doesn't just get dirty, then these are decisions that get made, and you don't have clean drinking water because of decisions about money that are made." Moore continued: "We were talking backstage about Flint. There are many Flints around this country. And it's not just that we have an environmental problem, but we have an economic problem where those people, in your case, in Alabama, and my case in Flint, where decisions get made where they say, 'You know what? These people, they aren't worth the investment, and they have no political power, and they don't buy candidates, and we don't have to do anything.'"

He captured my sentiments precisely.

The next morning, I received a call from Senator Cory Booker. He asked me to drop by his office before leaving for Alabama. Senator Doug Jones of Alabama was going to be there. This meeting was the first time Jones and I would come face-to-face since his 2018 election to the Senate in a race that had drawn national attention. Our initial meeting had taken place when he was candidate Jones, and it had not been pleasant.

A friend had held a fundraiser for Jones in Tuscaloosa. I attended and looked forward to meeting the candidate. After his presentation, I raised my hand and asked him what he planned to do about the raw sewage problem in Lowndes County. He told me that he had heard about it but was going to focus on the big problems and not the little problems. I pushed back and said, "Sen. Cory Booker thought it was important enough to come and visit, and so did the U.N. special rapporteur on extreme poverty." Jones dismissed me and went on to something else. I was disappointed. Now I had to choose between him—a Democratic candidate who did not seem to care about wastewater issues—and Roy Moore, the Republican former chief justice of the Supreme Court of Alabama who was accused of sexual misconduct with minors. His character issues did not align with my values. This was the kind of dilemma I often had to deal with. But instead of giving up, I made a call to Sen. Booker and told him what had happened. I felt I had to find a way to reach Jones. Several months later, I was meeting him in Booker's office.

As I walked in, the two men rose. I hugged Booker, whom I now considered a close friend. Jones shook my hand. We took our seats, and Jones and I talked. He told me he had been in the Rose Garden at the White House when General John Kelly, then White House chief of staff, had asked him what was going on in Lowndes County. I was delighted that we had gotten the attention of someone in the White House, but Jones didn't share my enthusiasm. I suspect that he was embarrassed by the attention, because he expressed concern that I had taken the media to see the wastewater problem.

I was not going to be shamed into shying away from the problem. I replied, "I will continue to take the media to see the waste situation firsthand as long as there is a problem." I told him to be prepared for other news stories to be broadcast nationally and internationally.

He backed down and asked, "What do you want me to do?" I knew that he had no idea about the problem, thinking back to my first time asking him about it when he was a candidate. It was time for him to learn. Two weeks later, I met him in Lowndes County.

Jones arrived in a dark SUV with two staffers. He wore blue jeans, and I remember thinking he looked as if he had just come from a hunting trip. He appeared tired but was attentive when we went to visit families and saw raw sewage on the ground around their homes. Charlie Mae Holcombe, someone I regularly took visitors to see, welcomed us to her home as she had greeted visitors so many times before. She told Jones about the wastewater problem she had experienced for at least twenty-eight years.

Jones seemed dubious when she said sewage flowed into her yard from the sewage lagoon across the street. He said he didn't see how that could occur, and he didn't believe she could be paying a wastewater fee and be using a septic tank. This reaction was common among people who had spent little time in rural communities. They don't understand that in some cases homes on municipal systems still have septic systems. Their waste is piped to a treatment center or, in this case, a lagoon. To Jones's credit, he asked to see the lagoon.

We drove through the open gate of the lagoon and walked around the stinking lake of effluent. A worker from the town drove up and began calling someone on his cell phone. I knew the city officials didn't like it when I took visitors to see the lagoon, but most times when I went there, no one was present. I told Jones I was afraid the situation could escalate. He walked over to the worker and introduced himself, and we had no problems as long as we were there. Then we went to the Lowndes Interpretive Center, our last stop. There, Jones learned that even the Interpretive Center, a building controlled by the federal government, had a failed septic system. The sewage flowed into the yard next to the property. The woman who lived next door said that when the system overflowed, she could not use the front door of her home. She'd have to walk through sewage to get there.

This never would have been allowed at a National Park Service site in an urban setting. Yet in rural America, it was being ignored. Policymakers and business leaders from around the country stop at the Lowndes Interpretive Center on their way to Selma and use the restroom. Little do they know that some of their waste may end up in this young woman's yard. Jones had become the first U.S. senator from Alabama, and the second senator since Booker's visit, to see it firsthand.

Since then, he has sponsored two of our congressional briefings.

The following month, the Equal Justice Initiative opened the first-ever national memorial to victims of lynchings in the United States. This idea was the brainchild of Bryan Stevenson. People came from around the nation to pay homage. There were three days of concerts, a prayer service, and panels with influential speakers addressing packed audiences. Among the presenters were Cory Booker, Rev. Barber, and former Vice President Gore. All three acknowledged Lowndes County and the raw sewage issue.

The event encapsulated so much of what had driven my work and my life for so long: the history of racial injustice, the current environmental injustice, and the moral and political aspects of the problems and solutions. It felt like a climactic moment for all those reasons—and the fact that I was among a community of doers and problem solvers whom I'd long admired.

One of the highlights for me was when Bryan asked me to have an onstage conversation with Al Gore about climate change and environmental justice. I was serving on the board of the Climate Reality Project, which Gore had founded. Bryan and I were delighted when Gore agreed to travel to Montgomery, present his famous slideshow on climate change that he's shown around the world, and take part in an open discussion.

We met in the greenroom before our presentation that morning. Gore had attended the events for all three days, from the concert by John Legend and Patti LaBelle to the prayer service at the memorial. As I prepared for our presentation, it felt like

I'd reached another milestone. I thought back to when I'd first met Karenna Gore in Selma, and then spoke with her father at Union Theological Seminary. Now we knew each other well enough to feel comfortable having a loosely structured conversation about subjects we both knew well. I had to take a deep breath. I closed my eyes and thought about how far I'd come and the enormity of what was about to happen.

In the middle of my reflection, Sen. Doug Jones came into the room with his wife, Louise. He greeted both Gore and me, and he introduced me to his wife. It was special for him to be present with us just before we went on stage, and I sincerely appreciated it. We posed for a picture to capture the moment, then Bryan joined us.

It was time for me to go to the stage for a sound check. Audience members were taking their seats in the sold-out auditorium. The stage manager told me the overflow room was full as well. I could see Sen. Booker sitting near the aisle in the front row, surrounded by fans waiting to take selfies with him. I took another deep breath and said a silent prayer, waiting until the big moment when I would introduce Al Gore.

Just as I did at Wheaton, I decided to speak without notes, because I wanted it to be authentic. I was proud that my daughter was also in the audience. She would get to see me in my professional persona. I introduced Al to loud applause. He would be speaking to admirers from around the nation. He began by acknowledging Sens. Booker and Jones, his daughter Karenna, and of course Bryan.

Before starting his slideshow, he gave a history of the environmental justice movement and traced its beginnings to Warren County, North Carolina, in the 1970s with a protest against hazardous waste that was being dumped in a low-income minority community. One of the first people involved in the movement was Rev. Barber's father, Al said.

Al eloquently tied together the big issues we'd been discussing for three days: from slavery's history and its scars to climate change and environmental justice. He discussed "broken systems," a phrase I thought aptly described the dirty truth about sewage and inequality in rural America. His slide presentation included our parasite study, emphasizing health inequities in marginalized and rural communities that will be worsened by climate change. He talked about the outbreaks of waterborne illnesses in the United States that follow major downpours, noting that those dramatic weather events also spread raw sewage and create conditions ripe for tropical diseases. He took that moment to acknowledge Dr. Paul Farmer, who was in the audience.

After the slide presentation, I rejoined Al onstage. We sat in comfortable gray chairs, and it was time for my "Oprah moment" as I moderated the discussion. It was a wide-ranging conversation, touching on political corruption, barriers to using renewable energy, climate gentrification, and water scarcity. Al spoke of the disconnect between public policy and public interest. "We have to reclaim the American democracy for the American people," he said.

Finally, I asked him, "How do we make sure that my grandson, who is two, will have a livable world?" He paused, seeming to collect himself before answering. I know he was thinking about his grandchildren and that this question resonated with every parent or grandparent who was present. He answered, "Our focus on short-term goals and overnight opinion polls [has] created the crisis that we are in. We have to get away from short-term thinking and look at the longer-term effects of what we are doing.

"We have to reform capitalism."

During the events of that week, I had an encounter that turned out to be life changing. It was my first face-to-face meeting with banker Kat Taylor from California, a woman who, with her husband, Tom Steyer, has thought a lot about reforming capitalism. They know the subject well as both hugely successful businesspeople and passionate social activists.

Kat and I were introduced through a text message by an EJI fellow named Justin Porter, who had majored in environmental science at Harvard. Justin, a Jackson, Mississippi, native, was extraordinarily bright, and I had become his Montgomery Mom during his stint at EJI. He was a friend of Kat's son Henry, and he thought Kat and I would have a lot to talk about.

Kat and I had several conversations, and she and Tom decided to come to Montgomery for the opening of the memorial. The day before the opening, she arrived, and we grabbed a late dinner. We agreed to meet the next day and go to the opening event.

The next evening I was with my friends, Walter Farrow, a retired veteran, and Sheila Frazier-Atchison, an actress and icon. Walter, Sheila, and I were dressed in after-five attire as Walter drove us to the Montgomery Performing Arts Center to attend a reception before the show began. All I knew was that I wanted to see John Legend. I was a fan. I didn't know the details of the full program, but I knew it would be a first-class affair full of historical remembrance.

The three of us were anticipating the evening when we felt a jolt from behind. A small SUV had been rammed in the rear by an oversized truck and then had hit us. The SUV was totaled, and its driver was hospitalized. We were badly shaken. Waiting for the police to arrive, I texted Kat to let her know that we had been in an accident. She called to ask for our location. She said she was out running and would find us.

During all the commotion, Kat jogged to the scene in her running clothes. She stayed with us until the reports were taken, and she drove our damaged car to her hotel. We were all a little bit in shock, but her kindness was like a balm, calming our nerves. We decided we weren't going to miss the chance to bear witness to this event, and we'd push through the pains we were all feeling if possible. I knew then that Kat was the kind of person I'd be blessed to have in my life. I'd find out later how right my instincts were.

Kat joined us at the reception, looking stunning. She said she wanted to introduce us to her husband, who was already at the reception. We began to walk around the room, meeting people as we navigated the "Who's Who" crowd. Eventually, we saw her husband holding court with a small group of people. She introduced us to Tom Steyer, the billionaire businessman who now devoted his life to environmental and social justice and would later run for president. We spent the rest of the evening and most of the next day with Kat and Tom and found them kind and down-to-earth. Before returning to California, Kat invited me to join her at the Mosaic Festival in Portland, Oregon, and to visit San Francisco for the first time.

Several weeks later, I was a guest in the home of Tom and Kat. Kat and I had a lot in common. We were close in age. We believed in social justice. We liked the same type of music, although she could sing, and I could not. We were both workaholics who loved our families. She was an excellent cook, and I consider myself a good cook too. She was great company.

While visiting her home, I received an email from an editor at the *New York Times* telling me an op-ed I had submitted would be published the next day after I reviewed the edits. I sat at Kat's dining room table, with her dogs for company, emailing back and forth with the editor until the piece was ready. The next afternoon, it went live on the *Times'* website, and then appeared in the following day's paper. The op-ed was entitled, "A County Where the Sewer Is Your Lawn."

I was elated. The *Times*' readership is huge and international. I'd taken Lowndes County's story to audiences of activists and government leaders, but this would give once voiceless people a chance to be heard by a mass audience.

A few weeks later, I was on a flight to Geneva, Switzerland, to attend the thirty-eighth session of the Human Rights Council. There, I would witness Dr. Philip Alston delivering his official report on his visit to the United States, including Lowndes County, and participate in a debate at the Graduate Institute in Geneva hosted by *The Guardian*. My travel companion was an old friend from college, Avril Harris, who is a realtor and community activist.

We decided to take a direct flight to Geneva from Dulles International Airport near Washington, DC. Avril told me that Geneva was similar in size to Montgomery. It had excellent public transportation, and most people spoke multiple languages, including English. I tried to sleep on the overnight flight, but to no avail. I passed the time watching *A Wrinkle in Time* and talking with Avril. We were both full of anticipation.

Geneva is a very modern city, and the U.N. grounds reminded me of a college campus or Capitol Hill in Washington, DC. Walking past the flags of all the member nations was a reminder of the historic mission of the U.N.—to foster cooperation and peace among nations. Unfortunately, our own country would be absent.

Our time in Geneva intersected with the withdrawal of the United States from the U.N.'s Human Rights Council. U.S. Ambassador Nikki Haley had just announced the departure with an interesting choice of words. "For too long," she said, "the Human Rights Council has been a protector of human rights abusers, and a cesspool of political bias." The word "cesspool" struck me as significant. That term and its variations were becoming a recurrent theme.

Six months prior, in January 2018, President Donald Trump, speaking to a group of senators about immigration, had reportedly asked why America would want immigrants from "all these shithole countries." At the time, I thought his choice of words showed his ignorance. He might have thought he was talking about poor, non-white countries, but he unknowingly described vast expanses of the United States that have their own American versions of "shitholes."

Now, the public conversation had turned to "cesspools."

As we entered the room where the Human Rights Council was meeting, my eyes went to the ceiling. The art was impressive. Otherwise, the room seemed somewhat ordinary, with representatives seated behind plaques with the names of their nations. Of course, I looked for the United States, but that seat was vacant. I moved to an area a few rows behind where the U.S. delegation would have been, joining another group from the United States that had also hosted Alston during his visit. Suspense and anticipation hung in the air as Alston began to speak.

"I note with regret that United States Ambassador Nikki Haley has characterized this Council as a cesspool and chosen to withdraw from it just days before my presentation," he said. "Speaking of cesspools, my report draws attention to those that I witnessed in Alabama as raw sewage poured into the gardens of people who could never afford to pay $30,000 for their own septic systems in an area remarkably close to the state capital. I concluded that cesspools need to be cleaned up and governments need to act. Walking away from them in despair, as in Alabama, only compounds the problems."

I sat there in disbelief that we had factored into this high drama on the world stage. It was as if wastewater was the understudy in the play and stole the show. We had defied the prediction that this issue wasn't sexy enough to attract attention.

Against all odds, a Black woman from Lowndes County had brought America's cesspools to the international human-rights arena.

Chapter 10

During one of my conversations with Kat Taylor, she asked if I would come with her to Allensworth, California. She told me that it was a community in California's San Joaquin Valley that was having water issues. I started researching it and discovered a fascinating history.

Allensworth is three hours from Los Angeles and four hours from San Francisco in a remote section of Tulare County, one of the most productive agricultural counties in the United States. It was named for Colonel Allen Allensworth, a former slave and army chaplain who founded the town in 1908 with four other settlers. They dreamed of a town where Black people could flourish, and for a time they succeeded. Hundreds of families arrived and built homes, a church, a school, and shops. The town had a library, post office, and its own form of government.

The settlers had big dreams. Rev. Allensworth wanted to build a vocational school modeled after Alabama's Tuskegee Institute. It would be the Tuskegee of the West, serving Black students. His proposal won support from state senators and representatives from Tulare and neighboring Fresno counties, but not the full California legislature. The failure to fund the vocational school wounded the town. This development would have provided a fantastic opportunity for African Americans from around the state.

There would be even more setbacks. California had no Jim Crow laws, so it must have seemed like a promising place to start a new life far from the racial terror of the South. But racism existed in other forms, and after several years it contributed to the end of the dream. A hard blow struck the town when the Santa Fe Railroad moved its Allensworth spur at the insistence of white neighbors.

That wasn't all. Seemingly abundant water had attracted the original settlers to Allensworth, but it wouldn't last. A drought, ever-increasing diversions of canal water to farmland, and a fast-growing state left Allensworth gasping for survival. The little town lacked the financial and political clout to claim its share from the white-run irrigation company that controlled water allocations in the area. As the water dried up, people moved away.

Col. Allensworth didn't live to see all this. He was killed in September 1914 by a couple of white men on a motorcycle who may have hit him intentionally. It was a sad irony that a man who did so much to escape the racist terror of the South would die in such a violent manner in California.

Despite the exodus, a few settlers stayed on, and the enclave of Allensworth managed to cling to life over the years. Then in 1974, the state of California bought some of the land within the original settlement and created Colonel Allensworth State Historic Park, with restored buildings to show visitors what the town was like when the vision was still alive.

There's another side of Allensworth, though. A few hundred people, largely immigrant farmworkers, live outside the state park, unable to drink the toxic water that flows from their taps. I was intrigued and thankful for a chance to visit a place that had many parallels with my own home. In Allensworth as in Lowndes County, dreams of a better life had given way to struggles for necessities. And in both places, climate change threatened to worsen a grim situation.

On the afternoon of October 11, 2018, I flew to San Francisco to meet Kat for the trip. Her friend, the actress Jane Fonda, would be joining us. My luggage did not arrive on my flight, so instead of going to Kat's house, I decided to stay near the airport. A long day got longer as I searched for a room on a night when most hotels seemed to be booked. By the time I found one, my bags still hadn't arrived. But being from Lowndes County, I knew how to wash my clothes by hand and hang them to dry so I could wear them the next day.

In the morning, I took an Uber to the airport and got my bag. Wanting to look my best, I changed clothes in the nearest bathroom. Shortly afterward, I received a call letting me know that Jane had arrived at the airport. I went to meet her in the baggage claim area.

When I introduced myself, Jane removed her sunglasses and looked me in the eye and smiled. I was stunned at how beautiful and warm she was. I blurted out, "My, you are beautiful!" I am generally not star-struck, and I did not want her to see me that way, but I was in awe of her fire, beauty, and years of social justice work. It was one of those moments when my past met my present. Here I was, a poor Black girl from Lowndes County, Alabama, meeting a Hollywood icon and activist. It was a great honor.

Jane and I met Kat curbside, and the three of us began our road trip to Allensworth. First, we stopped in Palo Alto, where Jane and Kat attended a business meeting. Later, we walked around the town square, and Kat showed us the pub where she had gone on her first date with Tom Steyer. With a long drive ahead of us, we ate at a restaurant nearby.

That gave us a chance to get acquainted, and as we started on the road, we were talking like old friends. About an hour and a half into the trip, I asked Kat to stop at a service station so I could use the bathroom. It was a sparsely populated area, and the sun was beginning to set. The bathroom was outside the station, which isn't always a good sign, but there were no other options, so we stood in line, the three of us, waiting our turn—a Hollywood star, a billionaire banker, and a Black woman from Lowndes County. Jane and Kat didn't bat an eye.

We stayed that night in an Airbnb. In the morning, Kat got up early and bought groceries. Jane and I met in the kitchen and fixed breakfast. We sat at the table discussing environmental issues, immigration, and voting. Jane was so authentic and our conversation so natural, I asked her if she would become a board member for the new organization we were forming to address environmental justice issues on a broader scale than ACRE did. To my surprise, Jane agreed. When Kat joined us in the kitchen, Jane told her she was my newest board member. I was elated, and even more so when Kat also agreed to join the board.

For the next phase of the trip, we joined a caravan that included a busload of additional guests going to Allensworth. Some of my friends were on the bus, and I rode with them. Among them were Felicia Gaston and her youth group from Marin City, whom I'd met through Kat at the opening of the National Memorial to Peace and Justice in Montgomery. Now we reconnected.

I looked out of the window as we traveled from Fresno to Allensworth. In new locations, I get a sense of place from watching the names of streets, roads, towns, and the terrain.

Taken together, they tell a story. I had a feeling of déjà vu when we passed a town called Selma. This Selma had a sign proclaiming it "the raisin capital of the world." From the bus, I noticed the rows and rows of almond trees. There were also cotton fields. It was clear that agriculture was the main driver of the economy.

Several months earlier, I had attended a conference where water policy was discussed. I'd heard about decisions around groundwater that heavily favored business and big agriculture over people. This trip would allow me to see firsthand how those policies and climate change affected access to water and wastewater treatment in California.

I'd heard that the landscape of the Central Valley has been irrevocably altered by agriculture and the drive to subject nature to the whims and needs of California's huge population and growth mentality. One of the most dramatic examples is the disappearance of Tulare Lake, once the largest freshwater lake west of the Mississippi. The Tachi tribe of the Yokut people, some seventy thousand strong at the peak of their population, had fished its waters and hunted along its shores for centuries. But with white settlers came the realization that the arid land of the valley, once the floor of a mighty inland sea, was unbelievably fertile. It just needed to be irrigated.

As more white settlers flocked to California, towns and cities needed water too. Rivers were dammed and canals were built to divert water that would have fed the lake. Then came the floods of 1938 and 1955, and more dams to harness nature and tame its unpredictability. Now the great Tulare Lake is no more. Shockingly, in some parts of the valley, land has subsided as much as thirty feet in the past century as the underground water table drops.

As we neared Allensworth, population 471, I saw trailers like the ones I regularly see in Lowndes County. They're a common symbol of rural poverty in any region. In this part of the San Joaquin Valley, the median household income is nearly two-thirds lower than the state's.

In Allensworth, we gathered in the gym of an elementary school. There, we met Denise and Kayode Kadara and Denise's brother, Kevin Hutson. Denise and Kevin's mother, Nettie Morrison, had moved her family to Allensworth in 1979. She worked hard to promote public awareness of the town's history and also to protect Allensworth from environmental threats such as corporate dairy operations that produce enormous quantities of animal waste and associated greenhouse gases. But she couldn't protect herself. She passed away from a condition her family suspected was tied to arsenic in the water. Her children and son-in-law carry on her activism. They teach sustainable farming practices on their land and advocate for clean water.

In Allensworth, the water that comes through residents' taps is piped from community wells that are contaminated with arsenic at levels too high for human consumption. Arsenic is a carcinogen that occurs naturally in certain soils, usually deep in the earth. High concentrations of arsenic in water have been linked to excessive groundwater pumping and the resulting subsidence of the earth.

Arsenic can be removed from water with the proper treatment, but little communities like Allensworth can't afford that solution. So unless a more affordable treatment process is developed or a government agency steps in to help with money, residents will continue having to buy water by the jug, bottle, or tank with their already meager incomes. Meanwhile, even though they can't drink the water from their taps, residents are still charged for it. Many homes don't have working septic systems.

And Allensworth is not alone. The San Joaquin Valley is

dotted with small rural communities whose wells are contaminated with arsenic, nitrates from fertilizer and animal waste, and other toxic substances.

It seemed to me that Allensworth looked like Lowndes County without water. Besides the dilapidated trailers, I immediately recognized another similarity: the deep green patches behind some homes that showed where raw sewage was pooling. Once again, I was witnessing the plight of low-income families whose infrastructure needs come last, even though they provide the labor that enriches others. This time, though, instead of Alabama, it was happening in wealthy California.

Allensworth serves as a cautionary tale for what happens to the poor and marginalized when there's competition for infrastructure dollars. It's an example of how rural communities are neglected and government fails to protect the powerless. If not for journalists, most notably at the *Fresno Bee*, few outside the poor communities that exist without clean water would know about their struggles. Even so, it's questionable how many Californians care. The state has been painfully slow to respond— officials have known about the arsenic since the 1960s. It's just not a priority. Sadly, this is nothing new.

As news of our work in Lowndes County spreads, I'm increasingly asked to visit other regions where wastewater issues persist unaddressed. I have been invited to Puerto Rico, Kentucky, Alaska, Hawaii, Illinois, and the Navajo Nation. My travels have opened my eyes to the fact that this is far from just a southern problem. It's happening throughout rural America, and in some places that aren't so rural. Sometimes it even happens in towns where people pay wastewater treatment fees to a management entity, close to urban centers. Centreville, Illinois, is one such location.

Earthjustice, one of our partners in the quest for sanitation equity, published an article about our collaboration in their magazine. Two attorneys who read the article reached out to me to discuss raw sewage issues in Centreville, an unincorporated area outside St. Louis, Missouri. Nicole Nelson is the founder and executive director of Equity Legal Services, and Kalila Jackson is a staff attorney with the Metropolitan St. Louis Equal Housing and Opportunity Council. They invited me to visit.

Centreville is approximately 95 percent African American. It's the most impoverished town in Illinois and one of the poorest in the United States. More than a third of its residents live below the poverty line. Many of the residents seeking help were over sixty years old. They relied on Social Security, Social Security disability checks, or their retirement pensions as their sole sources of income. I'd heard homes had been damaged by sewage backups and stormwater runoff, but I didn't know what to expect in this northern town. I was eager to see it firsthand.

I flew into St. Louis in the fall of 2019. The trip to Centreville from the airport was only about thirty minutes. Along the way, Kalila provided historical perspective. Located in St. Clair County, an area famous for environmental pollution, Centreville was typical of the places where residents lived with the short end of a trade-off with corporate polluters. Some people made money, but others, like Centreville's residents, were left with contaminated communities and lasting poverty.

My friend Walter Farrow accompanied me on the trip. Walter is a retired army sergeant major and a veteran of Afghanistan, Desert Storm, and Desert Shield. He wanted to learn more about environmental justice and had a deep desire to give back to society. We stopped at a restaurant for a late lunch and a meeting with members of the committee leading the community effort to address Centreville's wastewater problem. Our hosts were waiting for us. They included three co-presidents of the resident committee. Most of the residents present were retired and had lived in Centreville most of their adult lives. One was still working as a plumber. Each person shared stories about raw sewage entering their homes, fouling their yards, and flowing through ditches. After our working lunch, we set out to see the problems in person.

Kalila and Nicole were our guides. The passion with which they described the problem reminded me so much of Lowndes County residents and how we struggled to explain the wastewater problem to outsiders. I knew which questions to ask, and I also knew when to just listen as they tried to help us understand what we were about to see.

After lunch, they drove us to an area near Centreville and pulled off the road. They showed us ditches on both sides of the highway where runoff seemed to be flowing downhill from Belleville, a neighboring town. Our guides suspected it was a large part of the flooding problems residents were experiencing in Centreville.

The first thing I noticed when we entered the residential area of Centreville was the poor condition of the streets. Potholes were everywhere. On the edge of the roads, we saw exposed drainage pipes and pavement that was starting to collapse. I could tell they had a problem with runoff from stormwater, which is a form of wastewater. Erosion from flooding was evident everywhere. Kalila said flooding from rainstorms would often trap residents in their homes. Some had to be rescued by boats.

We visited a home that the original homeowner had moved out of in order to escape the chronic mess. I was able to follow a trail of raw sewage, dotted with toilet paper, that flowed through an indentation in the yard to the street. We saw sewage flowing through ditches as we toured neighborhoods. At one home, the owner talked about all the money she had put into renovations because of sewage flooding into her basement. All complained of their homes' losing value to the point they couldn't get loans to make repairs. They feared disease and wondered about the quality of their drinking water. Yet they all paid a wastewater fee to a utility.

The narrative that we had heard for so long in Lowndes County was that a management entity would ensure that the technology would continue to function and take the burden off the homeowner. Yet as I have seen in small towns in Lowndes County and other rural communities, managed systems are no better than onsite septic if the materials are substandard and the technology isn't suited for the area. The results are the same. In Centreville, I witnessed inequality underscored by environmental injustice, exacerbated by climate change, and perpetuated by poor policy. In each situation I have seen firsthand, the people in those forsaken communities were left to find solutions. If they had been corporations or prosperous businesses, they would have received public monies to help address the issue.

A pattern was beginning to emerge. This was a human-rights issue. As I had heard Reverend Barber and others say often, "people were treated like things and corporations were treated like people."

Even though I was increasingly aware of other suffering communities, I had reason to believe we were getting attention from people who could help. Two noteworthy events had occurred before my visit to Centreville. One was my testimony before the Congressional Subcommittee on Water Resources and the Environment in 2019. The hearing, chaired by Representatives Grace F. Napolitano (D-California) and ranking member Bruce Westerman (R-Arkansas), was labeled "The

Clean Water State Revolving Fund: How Federal Infrastructure Investment Can Help Communities Modernize Water Infrastructure and Address Affordability Challenges."

I brought with me Brandon Hunter, an engineer and PhD candidate from Duke; Sekita Grant from the Emerson Collective; and Jenifer Collins from Earthjustice. I'd submitted my written testimony in advance and was prepared to respond to questions and provide testimony.

The room was smaller than I'd envisioned. I was seated at a table with a number of other speakers—mayors, municipal utilities officials, engineers, and academics. They were Mayor David A. Condon, from Spokane, Washington, on behalf of the U.S. Conference of Mayors; John Mokszycki, water and sewer superintendent for Greenport, New York, on behalf of the National Rural Water Association; Andrew Kricun, executive director/chief engineer of the Camden County Municipal Utilities Authority, Camden, New Jersey, on behalf of the National Association of Clean Water Agencies; Professor Jill Heaps, assistant professor of law at Vermont Law School; and my friend Maureen Taylor, state chairperson of the Michigan Welfare Rights Organization. I knew Maureen from our work together with the National Coalition for the Human Right to Water and Sanitation and the New Poor People's Campaign. She has been fighting the water affordability crisis in Detroit for a long time. Residents there have been plagued with numerous water shutoffs. When there is no access to water in the home, there is no access to sanitation.

Everyone testifying made an argument for reauthorizing the Clean Water State Revolving Fund administered by the Environmental Protection Agency. The program gives communities an independent source of low-cost financing for water and wastewater infrastructure development. Each of us presented a unique perspective of water and sanitation access, but Andrew Kricun spoke for all of us when he said, "Your ZIP code shouldn't determine if you have safe wastewater or not."

I listened attentively until it was my turn to read the testimony I'd written the night before. I turned on my microphone and began:

I am the rural development manager for the Equal Justice Initiative in Montgomery, Alabama. I am also a practitioner in residence at the Franklin Humanities Institute at Duke University, a senior fellow at the Center for Earth Ethics at Union Theological Seminary, the founder of the Alabama Center for Rural Enterprise, and the Center for Rural Enterprise and Environmental Justice.

I grew up in Lowndes County, Alabama, which is located along the route from Selma to Montgomery. As a child in the 1960s and '70s, I used an outhouse and a slop jar before my family eventually installed indoor plumbing. I left the area to achieve an education, and upon returning to Alabama in 2000, I was surprised at the disparities that still existed in rural wastewater treatment and access to public infrastructure funds.

Since 2002, I have visited homes with wastewater failures at all levels. I first began meeting with people about this problem in the early 2000s as people were threatened with or arrested for not being able to afford onsite wastewater treatment. Yes, it is a crime in this country if you cannot provide wastewater treatment. Many of the community members had resorted to unpermitted, alternative methods like straight piping to discharge raw sewage from their homes or disconnecting failing septic systems to keep the sewage from coming back into their homes.

CATHERINE COLEMAN FLOWERS

And while the arrests have decreased, the threat remains.

I have visited homes with onsite systems that fail each time it rains, and the sewage comes back into the homes through either the toilet, bathtub, or both. In one town, citizens pay a wastewater treatment fee, yet they still have sewage backing up into their homes and yards. A neighborhood is bordered by a sewage lagoon, a cheap solution generally used in poor, rural communities. In addition to the stench from the pond of raw sewage, their tanks must be pumped as often as three times a week to remove wastewater from their yards or their homes. Children are unable to play in their yards due to raw sewage on the ground. This is not what people expect to see in the United States.

In 2009 I was bitten by mosquitoes swarming a pool of raw sewage. My body broke out in a rash that doctors could not identify. I later reached out to Dr. Peter Hotez of the National School of Tropical Medicine, which culminated in a peer-reviewed study that was published in 2017. The study found that over 30 percent of Lowndes County residents tested were found to have hookworm and other tropical parasites long thought to have been eradicated from the U.S.

Inadequate wastewater is not just a Lowndes County or an Alabama problem. It is estimated that more than 20 percent of the country uses onsite wastewater, reaching 40 percent or more in areas with large rural populations. Up to half of the septic systems in the U.S. don't work properly or fail at some point. By some estimates, 65 percent of the land in the U.S. cannot support septic systems.

It is time for Congress to act to address this widespread

problem, beginning with acknowledging the problem more broadly, gathering more information, especially through the census, and eliminating policies that criminalize residents for being unable to afford wastewater treatment. In addition, I invite all of you to visit rural areas of America to see these issues firsthand.

Then I outlined the steps that must be taken to address unequal access to basic infrastructure:

Congress should further use its oversight powers to ensure that investments in addressing this problem are meaningful. Specifically, it is critical that:

- Funding should consider the realities of climate change, community input, and the unique geography of an area.
- Funding must also go to those who need it most and cannot afford wastewater treatment or upgrades without assistance.
- And finally, if federal funding is used to continue to design and permit failing systems, the state entities that approved those systems should be held accountable instead of the individual homeowners.

Rural communities should no longer be left behind. Congress must begin addressing this problem now, while also looking at technological solutions for the new future of wastewater. If we can treat wastewater in outer space, it is not unrealistic to see a time when one can go to a hardware store and purchase an onsite wastewater treatment system. This is an opportunity to remove the shame associated with discussing wastewater treatment failures and instead focus on sustainable solutions not only in Alabama, but throughout the United States.

Many of the subcommittee members offered comments after the testimony ended. The ranking member, Representative Westerman, talked about the outhouse in the rural church that he attended as a child. Representative Doug LaMalfa talked about rebuilding part of his district after the Camp Fire, the most destructive fire in California history, in 2018. He talked about the town of Paradise, which was completely destroyed in the fire. I was encouraged by his vision of rebuilding Paradise and other destroyed areas using innovative technologies.

Another member of the subcommittee talked about raw sewage and sanitation inequality in his district. Representative Anthony Delgado, a forty-two-year-old Rhodes scholar, Harvard-trained lawyer, and former rapper, represents New York's 19th District. He characterized his district, which stretches throughout the Hudson Valley and Catskills regions, as the most rural in the state. He spoke about the lack of sanitation in his area. Once I would have been surprised, but by then I knew that wastewater problems occurred all throughout the United States.

I left the hearing feeling a sense of victory because of the consensus on both sides of the aisle about the need to address access to wastewater treatment throughout rural America. We still need to see whether this consensus will translate into action.

Several weeks later, I gave congressional briefings alongside my Columbia University collaborators, Inga Winkler and JoAnn Ward Kamuf. The briefings were hosted on both the House and Senate sides of the Hill. Each briefing room was packed beyond capacity, with staffers and activists seeking to interact with us afterward.

We presented a report we co-authored titled "Flushed and Forgotten: Sanitation and Wastewater in Rural Communities in the U.S." Inga and JoAnn have backgrounds in human rights that were very helpful in providing a framework for government action. They surmised the inequities were largely the result of government inaction. The report zeroed in on the lack of sanitation equity in rural communities in Alaska, Appalachia, Louisiana, Michigan, Mississippi, North Carolina, Ohio, Puerto Rico, and Texas.

People stayed long after the briefings ended and asked questions. Staffers told me that their representative or senator was deeply interested in this issue. We even were covered by *Buzz-Feed*. I believe policymakers were finally listening.

In October 2019, I was joined by Jane Fonda, Kat Taylor, and an additional board member, entrepreneur and activist Khaliah Ali, to officially announce the Center for Rural Enterprise and Environmental Justice. We gathered with supporters before newspaper and television reporters near the Confederate memorial in front of the Hayneville courthouse to explain our vision:

- To educate policymakers, academics, activists, and the public about the infrastructure needs of rural communities.
- To promote research in rural communities to expose health issues associated with air, water, and soil contamination.
- To engage college students in real-life situations, away from the classroom, developing a new generation of human-rights leaders.

Jane told reporters about the conditions she'd seen in Lowndes County and the bigger implications. "As the climate crisis gets worse, the problems that we saw today . . . are going to get worse," she said. "And one of the things that the center is working on is to develop the technology to deal with the sewage situations in rural areas."

I explained how we will use the lessons we learned in Alabama to help other communities around the country, including Allensworth and Centreville. Then Khaliah spoke.

"To work underneath, beneath, and with a group of women that are inspired by not just success but doing what is right in the world is really humbling for me," she said. "As the daughter of boxer Muhammad Ali, I couldn't think of a better way to stand here today and curate my father's legacy and be a part of what's happening here in Alabama."

The location of the news conference was significant. It was the same courthouse where an all-white jury had acquitted Tom Coleman for the cold-blooded killing of seminarian Jonathan Daniels. It was the same courthouse where I'd stood before a judge to save a young man from jail for his inability to buy a septic system for his family, when I was just learning about the problem. It's where I started to find my voice as an environmental activist.

There was a lot of history there, much of it painful and ugly. But there I was, with these dynamic, accomplished women beside me, preparing to write a new chapter in history. This chapter would be about human rights and dignity for all people. I could never have imagined it, but on that day, I felt like we could move mountains together. The world was going to hear more from us.

Not long after that day in Hayneville, another development came that filled me with joy and hope. This one was especially close to my heart.

Kat Taylor provided funds for a new mobile home for Pamela Rush and her family. No longer will Pam trap opossums and stuff rags into holes in the mold-infested walls of her home. She will still be poor, but she and her children will live safely in an energy-efficient home that's up to code and complete with a working septic system. Pam is joyful about her home, and she continues to sacrifice her own privacy to speak about the wastewater woes of Lowndes County. She was featured in *Time* magazine in February 2020, and has become the face of poverty in the rural South.

Getting a septic system installed for her was a case study in how complex the issue is in Lowndes County and why it is an expensive option for many there. While doing the perc test, the engineer struck water while digging just twenty inches into the ground. Because the water table was so high, Pam would need an engineered system. The first bid received for the installation of the system on a half-acre of land near where she currently lives was $28,000. That shows why so many of her neighbors are straight-piping. It also underscores the need for affordable technologies.

The fact is that there is no one-size-fits-all wastewater system. What works in one kind of soil won't function for long in another. We have to keep searching for new technology and new methods of disposing of human waste. I believe we will find solutions if we can direct the energies of academics, business, government, and philanthropy toward finding them, and that's where public policy comes in: to make this issue a priority, set standards for how we will live in the United States, and provide incentives for innovative solutions.

The United Nations considers access to sanitation to be a fundamental human right essential to health and dignity. It's taken me a while to realize just how many Americans lack that right. If you'd asked me a few years ago what I did, I'd have said I was an environmental justice activist. I wanted justice for the poor Black people of Alabama who had no means for rectifying a horrible situation that forced them to live in third-world conditions. Now, however, I understand that the issue affects all kinds of people regardless of race or geography.

I'll fight for better wastewater treatment technologies and fairer public policies for the white people living along the increasingly saturated Florida coastline, the Native Americans on reservations out west, Alaskans on the tundra, Ohioans, Michiganders, and Long Islanders, just as much as I will for my home county in Alabama. I will fight for people of color, immigrant communities, and even those who are well off but without functioning wastewater infrastructure. You shouldn't have raw sewage running back into your home or in your yard, period.

This shouldn't be a partisan issue. Although Democrats are the ones proposing legislation now, I'll never forget that some of my earliest help came from two conservatives, Bob Woodson and then Alabama Senator Jeff Sessions. When we work together, the United States can use its political clout, business acumen, engineering expertise, and wealth to fix the problem, and I'm working hard to help make that happen.

But when you have a president who makes comments about "shithole countries" while we have people living next to cesspools right here in this country, clearly there is no correlation between reality and what some people perceive it to be. Perhaps shining a spotlight on conditions that American citizens are forced to live in will start to bring about change, not just in Alabama, but also in rural and even suburban and urban areas across the country—and the world.

COVID-19, the disease caused by the novel coronavirus, has magnified the impacts of poverty, climate change, health disparities, and the lack of adequate sanitation in marginalized communities around the world. For more than eighteen years, I have sought to expose America's dirty secret, people living among raw sewage. The solutions have not come fast enough to ensure water and sanitation equality for all. Now COVID-19 has illustrated that it is a problem that can no longer be ignored. It has been suggested that the virus shows up in sewage and can be used as an indicator of the level of contagion in a city or community. The areas plagued for decades by the lack of wastewater are now also struggling with a modern-day plague.

America, we *can* do better. Everyone has a role to play, a way to contribute. This is my appeal to each of you to get involved in the pursuit of environment, climate, and wastewater justice.

I'm confident we can muster the imagination, innovation, and will to find solutions. I know it's possible because of what I've seen in my lifetime. I grew up in a time when Black people couldn't even vote. Now we've had a Black president. Montgomery, once a slave-trading center, finally elected its first Black mayor in 2019. Change that once seemed unthinkable is happening now.

I'm inspired by the passion of young people fighting for the health of our planet, most famously sixteen-year-old Greta Thunberg from Sweden. If you look at history, all significant movements and all significant changes are led by young people. They push us to do more, and I'm grateful to them. But there's also my friend, eighty-two-year-old Jane Fonda, who spent four months in Washington, DC, leading demonstrations, sometimes getting arrested, every Friday on the steps of the Capitol to raise awareness about climate change.

Anyone can be an activist, even a little Black girl from Lowndes County, Alabama. I hope my story inspires others to stand up when they see injustice. You never know where it might lead, no matter where you start. Initially, I got involved because that's how I was raised. Now, I'm involved because of my grandson. He's three years old. If we don't do the right thing, he won't have a future.

I think often of the Seventh Generation philosophy attributed to the Iroquois people. It holds that when we make important decisions, we must think not of ourselves, but rather of the children yet to come. We should think ahead for seven generations.

Those seven generations—and more—depend on what we do today.

Epilogue

COVID-19 swept through Lowndes County like a brushfire. In a sadly familiar pattern, poor people, and especially poor Black people, fell victim in alarming numbers. Elsewhere, the most brazen political leaders actually called for people to die for the economy. In Lowndes County, that's exactly what has happened. People are dying to save the very economic and social structures that trap them in poverty. After all, the poor are essential workers.

It wasn't long before Lowndes County had the highest per capita death rate for COVID in Alabama. Some people were infected at the factories, warehouses, nursing homes, or stores where they worked. They didn't have the luxury of telecommuting. Others caught it from family members who didn't know they had the virus or had no means of social distancing. They couldn't afford to check in to a motel. They had no second homes to retreat to.

In the absence of coherent public policy, people did what they could to help each other, leaving food and other supplies on the front porches of those who were infected. In one of our last conversations, Pamela Rush told me she was fixing some greens for a sick relative. At that time, we had acquired her new mobile home but the move we'd anticipated with such joy had been delayed.

Then, like a heat-seeking missile, the coronavirus zeroed in on Pam. She fought for her life on a ventilator for days, but she lost her last battle. The official cause of death was COVID, but the underlying causes of her suffering were poverty, environmental injustice, climate change, race, and health disparities. They would never be listed on a death certificate.

I felt powerless, unable even to visit Pam in the hospital in Birmingham where she'd been taken. Just a few months earlier I'd been in the same hospital with pneumonia and other complications from what should have been a routine surgery. My family and friends kept me company in the hospital, even spending nights there with me. That was before COVID, when visitors were still allowed. Pam, on the other hand, was isolated in the intensive care unit. Her family was not permitted at her bedside.

My heart ached for her and for them. I turned to Reverend Barber and Reverend Carolyn Foster, who head the New Poor People's Campaign in Birmingham, and arranged for them to get updates from the hospital staff and connect with Pam's family. At one point the hospital asked for a picture of Pam, maybe so the staff could see her as she was before COVID. I sent pictures of her with Senator Bernie Sanders and Reverend Barber. I wanted them to know this struggling patient was an important woman.

Before COVID, we thought we had a solution to Pam's plight. After years of living in horrible conditions, Pam had learned she and her children would finally have a livable home with a working septic system. Kat Taylor provided funds for CREEJ to get Pam a clear title on her property, and to work with Clayton Homes to acquire a safe, more energy-efficient home.

Sadly, Pam never got to live in her new home. She had seen it on the lot, but one obstacle after another had kept her family from actually moving in. We knew a wastewater system for her half-acre lot would be expensive to install but we learned it would take up a third of her property and be prohibitively expensive to maintain, requiring a constant supply of electricity. We were advised to seek other options. The last thing we wanted to do was to take her out of one trap and place her in another. Pam was told that if she could purchase an adjacent half-acre of property, she could obtain a septic that would cost less to maintain.

It began to feel like a series of trap doors. Each time one was opened, another would emerge. Then came the virus, stopping us in our tracks, delaying our efforts to find a solution as the state bureaucracy essentially shut down. And then the virus came for Pam.

In the end, it didn't matter that Pam had opened her life and shown the world what inequality looks like, or that some of the most influential Americans had walked through her home and left in disbelief. Billionaires had crossed her threshold. Alabama senator Doug Jones climbed her rickety front steps. Senator Bernie Sanders told her story in a video shown across the nation. He promised to work on policies to address her problems. But that would take time that Pam didn't have.

It didn't even matter that Pam had testified before Congress or that she'd become a face of the New Poor People's Campaign. The forces of structural poverty were too strong.

But it could still matter, if not to Pam, then to others. I'm hoping Pam's children will live in the home and enjoy the better life she envisioned for them.

The rest depends on all of us. My wish is that Pamela's life, activism, and death will move us to work for a just system that provides affordable wastewater treatment and decent housing for the rural poor. In Pam's name, for her children and the children of this nation, we must demand technological and policy solutions to wastewater inequities.

The first half of 2020 has brought tragedy, but it's also inspired change in the most amazing ways. Our country has been forced to reckon with its history of racial injustice. Senseless murders have brought us to the point that Black Lives Matter is a rallying cry in communities large and small. And a day came that I never expected. As Confederate statues toppled around the South, Lowndes County commissioners finally voted to remove the monument that stood for so long before the county courthouse.

When the news broke, a white friend texted me, jubilant that the monument was coming down. She mentioned that some of her relatives' names were on that monument. I replied that some of mine are on it too. I won't be sorry to see them go.

Not all monuments to injustice are built of stone. Others exist in practices and institutions, actions and inactions that undermine the dream of equality. To some, those monuments are invisible. To me, they're as real as the sewage that pools behind Pam Rush's trailer.

It's time to dismantle those monuments too.

Acknowledgments

A special thank you:

To Bryan Stevenson, whose shared experience and support helped create a wastewater revolution.

To those civil rights heroes from Lowndes County who have gone on to heaven: my parents, the Stricklands, the Jacksons, Bob Mants, Sarah Logan, and Gardenia White.

My Lowndes County family and friends. I will always love you and do what I can as a native to help bring first-world infrastructure to all.

Thank you to Stephanie Wallace, Marilyn Dice, Jeff Hall, Sandy Oliver, Ruby Rudolph, Mary McDonald, Betty Shabazz, Patricia Means, Aaron Thigpen, Stephen Thigpen, Antony Poole, and Yvonne Jones for helping to collect and organize the information on the wastewater problem in Lowndes County.

To my brothers, sister, nieces, nephews, and cousins who are constantly giving me words of encouragement.

To my sister and prayer partner, Lynda Black.

To Dr. Peter Hotez and Dr. Rojelio Mejia for trusting my theory and proving it to be real.

To my friend Michael Graham. Thank you for all of your advice.

To Charlie Mae Holcomb for always standing ready to witness for those afraid to do so, and opening her home to senators, pastors, and a former vice president of the United States.

To John Jackson, my brother in the movement for most of my life.

To Betsy Lumbye, the writer from the San Joaquin Valley who helped me shape this vision. To Mark Arax for connecting me to Betsy.

To my agent, Michelle Tessler, and the awesome publishing team at The New Press.

To all who have helped me realize the vision of telling my story and who support the goal of sanitation for all.

About the Author

Catherine Coleman Flowers is the founder of the Center for Rural Enterprise and Environmental Justice and since 2008 has been the rural development manager at the Race and Poverty Initiative of the Equal Justice Initiative. She lives in Montgomery, Alabama.

Publishing in the Public Interest

Thank you for reading this book published by The New Press. The New Press is a nonprofit, public interest publisher. New Press books and authors play a crucial role in sparking conversations about the key political and social issues of our day.

We hope you enjoyed this book and that you will stay in touch with The New Press. Here are a few ways to stay up to date with our books, events, and the issues we cover:

- Sign up at www.thenewpress.com/subscribe to receive updates on New Press authors and issues and to be notified about local events
- Like us on Facebook: www.facebook.com/newpress books
- Follow us on Twitter: www.twitter.com/thenewpress
- Follow us on Instagram: www.instagram.com/thenew press

Please consider buying New Press books for yourself; for friends and family; or to donate to schools, libraries, community centers, prison libraries, and other organizations involved with the issues our authors write about.

The New Press is a 501(c)(3) nonprofit organization. You can also support our work with a tax-deductible gift by visiting www.thenewpress.com/donate.

The Studs and Ida Terkel Award

On the occasion of his ninetieth birthday, Studs Terkel and his son, Dan, announced the creation of the Studs and Ida Terkel Author Fund. The Fund is devoted to supporting the work of promising authors in a range of fields who share Studs's fascination with the many dimensions of everyday life in America and who, like Studs, are committed to exploring aspects of America that are not adequately represented by the mainstream media. The Terkel Fund furnishes authors with the vital support they need to conduct their research and writing, providing a new generation of writers the freedom to experiment and innovate in the spirit of Studs's own work.

Studs and Ida Terkel Award Winners

Lawrence Lanahan, *The Lines Between Us: Two Families and a Quest to Cross Baltimore's Racial Divide*

Janet Dewart Bell, *Lighting the Fires of Freedom: African American Women in the Civil Rights Movement*

David Dayen, *Chain of Title: How Three Ordinary Americans Uncovered Wall Street's Great Foreclosure Fraud*

Aaron Swartz, *The Boy Who Could Change the World: The Writings of Aaron Swartz* (awarded posthumously)

Beth Zasloff and Joshua Steckel, *Hold Fast to Dreams: A College Guidance Counselor, His Students, and the Vision of a Life Beyond Poverty*

Barbara J. Miner, *Lessons from the Heartland: A Turbulent Half-Century of Public Education in an Iconic American City*

Lynn Powell, *Framing Innocence: A Mother's Photographs, a Prosecutor's Zeal, and a Small Town's Response*

Lauri Lebo, *The Devil in Dover: An Insider's Story of Dogma v. Darwin in Small-Town America*